The A to Z Book of Birds

An ABC for Young Bird Lovers

By Michael P. Earney

The A to Z Book of Birds – An ABC for Young Bird Lovers

Copyright © 2013, 2020 by Michael P. Earney All rights reserved. No part of this publication may be reproduced, stored in a retrieval system or transmitted in any way by any means, electronic, mechanical, photocopy, recording or otherwise without the prior permission of the author except as provided by USA copyright law.

Paperback: 978-1-941345-69-6
Hardcover: 978-1-941345-68-9
Second Edition

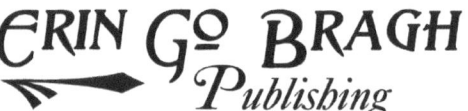

Canyon Lake, TX
www.ErinGoBraghPublishing.com

Cover watercolor painting of Scissor-tailed Flycatcher (*Tyrannidae*) and Red-necked Grebe (*Podicipedidae*) by Michael Earney.

Cover design, book design and layout by Michael Earney and Lynn Amos.

Authors Note: The A to Z Book of Birds, the first in the A to Z series, was published in 2014. The second in the series, The A to Z Book of Weeds and other useful Plants, and all the subsequent books, contained a poem, this second edition contains two poems and the title has been added to the spine, something the original publisher said couldn't be done. The series has seen some changes, The A to Z Book of Cats has artwork by children, in addition to my work, and there is even a drawing by my granddaughter Elowen.

Cool Fact: Every book in the series contains material that cannot be found elsewhere!

Dedication:

For Miles and Elowen

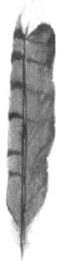

For the Birds

*Trills, coos, tweets, and chatters greet the dawn
birds in the sky, birds in the trees, birds on the lawn.
The sound of birdsong brightens every day
though less and less, it's sad to say
The Dodo and that pigeon, gone, and countless others too.
No one's to blame, but me and you.
Another is your kitty cat,
birds disappear, while cats grow fat.
herbicides and pesticides contaminate the food birds eat,
windmills, windows, cars and planes, their ranks deplete.
It's true, the Whooping Crane's back from the brink,
but other species see their numbers shrink.
The Condor that once soared on high,
it seems as though its end is nigh.
The Heron at the water's edge, the wise Owl calling in the night,
the Eagle and the Hummingbird, their future isn't looking bright.
Now, you and I can turn this thing around,
raise up your voice and make a sound.
Tell those who great decisions make,
to "Save the Birds!" Our very way of life's at stake.*

Michael P. Earney 2019

What the Flock

*A kettle of Hawks circling high in the sky
looks down on a gaggle of Geese
as a paddling of ducks passes by,
near a sedge of Cranes, that we hope will increase,
with that ballet of Swans, pray they'll never cease.
For that murmuration of Starlings, we've nothing to fear,
like a quarrel of sparrows, they'll always be here.
An unkindness of Ravens, a building of Rooks, a murder of Crows
they're all rather dull, as a flamboyance of Flamingos easily shows.
Still, even a puddling of Mallards outshines that dark three.
As a bright charm of Goldfinches sing-along from a tree,
across the wide lake, and its asylum of Loons,
an exaltation of Larks joins in with their tunes.
Then, a deceit of Lapwings makes a cast of Jays scold,
that's a tiding to Magpies, best not be too bold.
Should a banditry of Chickadees give a bad name to fowls,
the judging we'll leave to the wisdom of Owls.
Now, for those among you who think birds only flock,
I'm sure that the foregone has been quite a shock.
Still, there are only so many could say that I fail
If we come to the end with a covey of Quail.*

Michael P. Earney 2019

Acknowledgements:

My thanks to all the family and friends that fed and housed me during the process of producing this book. For input and encouragement, T.J. Cole, Jason Muñoz, Carol Elliott, my son Miles for introducing me to birding, all the bird illustrators before me, and especially thanks to Lynn Amos for getting the whole thing into the excellent (if I do say so myself) form it now has.

Michael P. Earney – August 9, 2014

Introduction:

The fossilized skeleton of a bird about the size of a crow, found in a Bavarian limestone quarry, has been determined to have lived one-hundred and forty-million years ago. It is estimated that between that time and the present up to two million species of birds existed. They have been gradually declining ever since. There are now approximately eight-thousand seven-hundred species. The spread of human beings to every corner of the globe has had the most devastating effect on bird populations: birds are shot, trapped, snared, or otherwise exterminated; their habitat destroyed or invaded and exploited. The amazing diversity and beauty of birds will continue to fascinate us, even as they disappear. Those that call themselves bird-lovers will hopefully make the effort to see that, as individuals, they influence their families, neighbors, corporations and governments to preserve wildlife and their habitat, and know that in so doing they are contributing to the betterment of all life on the planet.

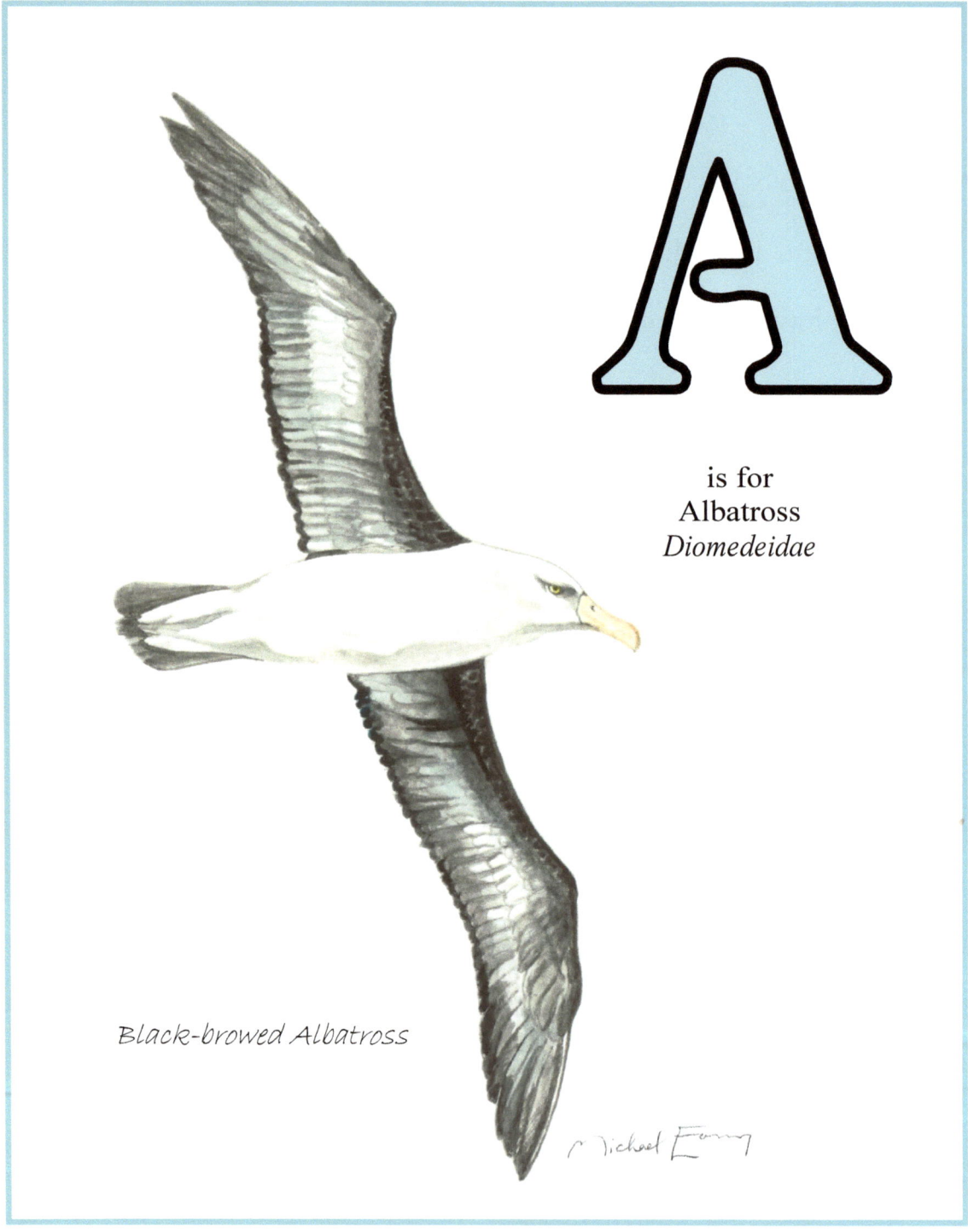

Albatrosses glide on the winds of the oceans, their long narrow wings allow them to stay aloft for months alighting only to feed and drink (they drink seawater). Of the 13 species only three breed north of the equator, but over half a million Laysan Albatrosses nest on the outer-most islands of Hawaii where they were slaughtered for feathers to stuff pillows and mattresses. To stop this President Theodore Roosevelt designated these islands a wildlife preserve in 1909. The Short-tailed Albatross, largest in the North Pacific has a wingspan reaching 13 feet. Almost wiped out by plume hunters, this rare bird now nests again on Torishima Islet, south of Tokyo.

Cool Fact: In the "Rime of the Ancient Mariner," a poem by Samuel Taylor Coleridge, after a sailor kills an albatross the wind drops and the ship cannot sail; the sailors begin to die of thirst. The sailor blamed for this disaster has the dead bird hung around his neck as punishment. Having an *'albatross around one's neck'* means feeling guilt, shame or anxiety.

What other birds' names start with A?

B is for Booby *Sulidae*

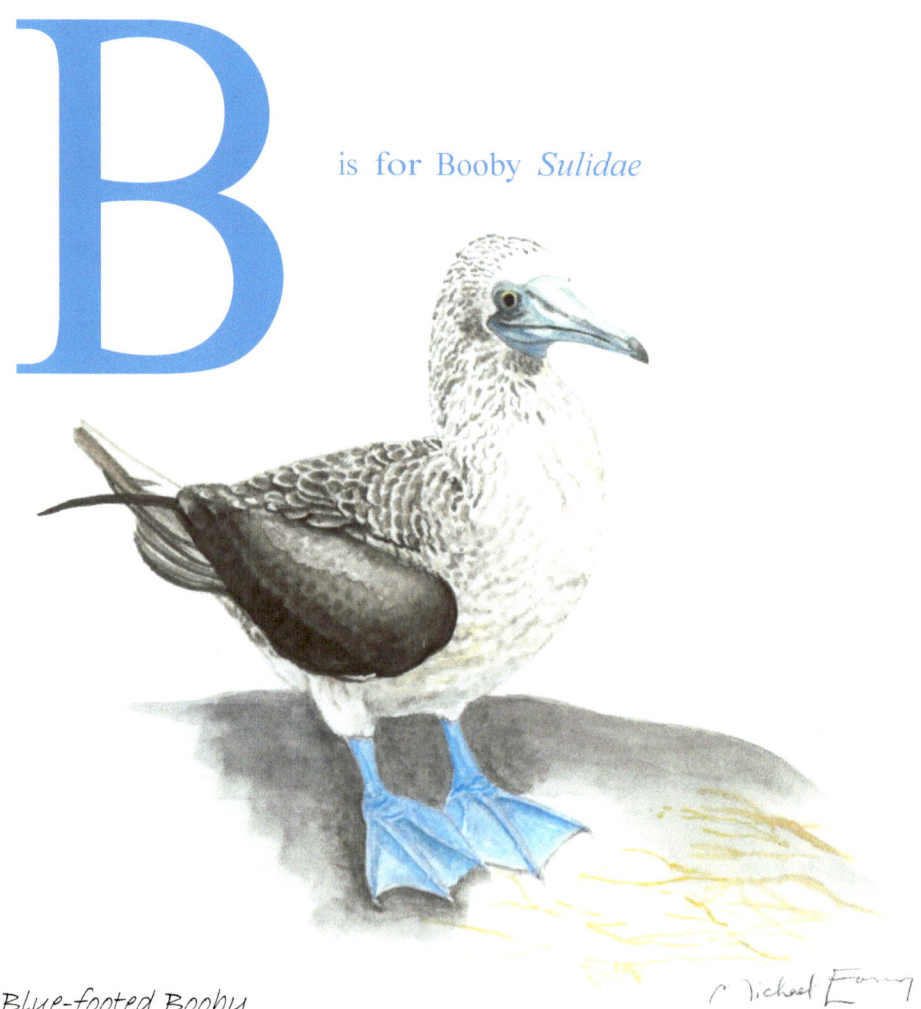

Blue-footed Booby

Booby comes from the Spanish *bobo*, dunce. They were called this because they never seemed to learn that man is their enemy. There is the Brown Booby, the Blue-faced Booby, the Blue-footed and the Red-footed, plus two others. Like many seabirds, boobies plunge from great heights for fish. Though they have very strong necks, it is the air sacs under their skin that cushion the impact of their dives. Instead of spearing fish with their straight sharp bills, they seize them from beneath as they return to the surface. When they landed on sailing ships they were easily caught and eaten by hungry sailors.

Cool Fact: Unlike its relatives, who nest on bare rock, the Red-footed Booby builds its nest in the treetops and feeds not by day but by night on flying fish and squid.

What other birds' names start with B?

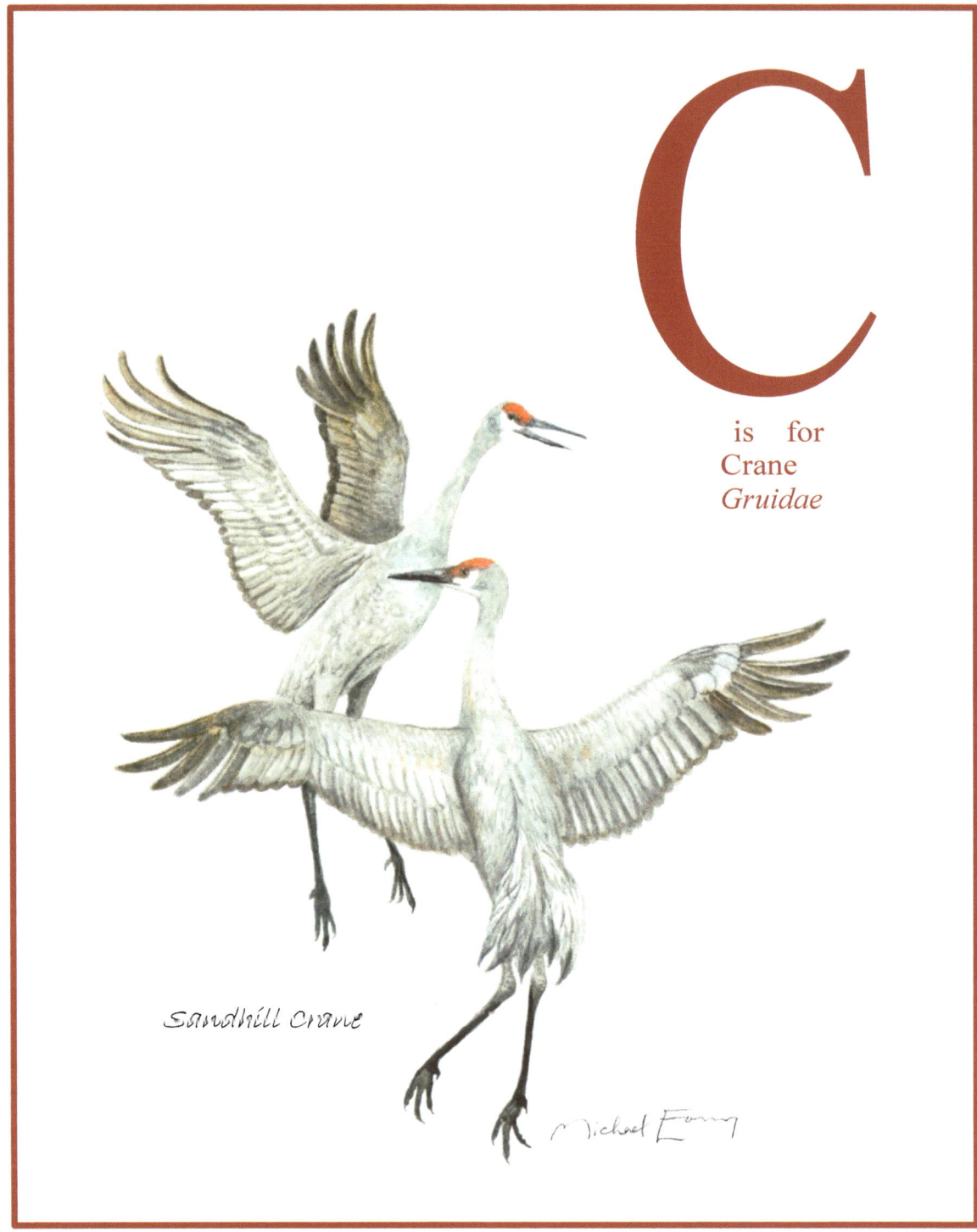

Cranes have been around for 40-60 million years, they can fly over mountains, live for over 60 years and, in America, fly each year from near the Arctic Circle to Texas and back. The Whooping Crane, tallest bird in North America, was down to 15 individuals in 1937. Thanks to great effort there are now around 500, but are still highly endangered and threatened with extinction. There are 15 species worldwide. The Sarus Crane of Asia is the tallest at five feet nine inches. The beautiful Black-crowned Crane and the Demoiselle Crane are the smallest at three feet and at thirty inches, respectively. Although revered in some countries, all cranes are in danger worldwide.

Cool Fact: The orizuru (folded crane) is the most classical and probably best known of all Japanese origami. Renzuru (conjoined cranes) is multiple cranes folded from a single sheet of paper.

What other birds' names start with C?

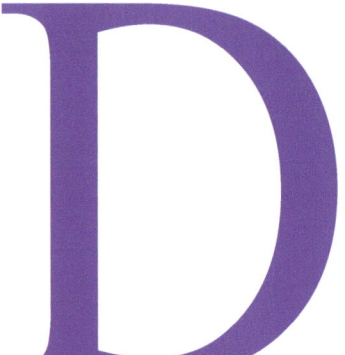

D is for Duck
Anatidae

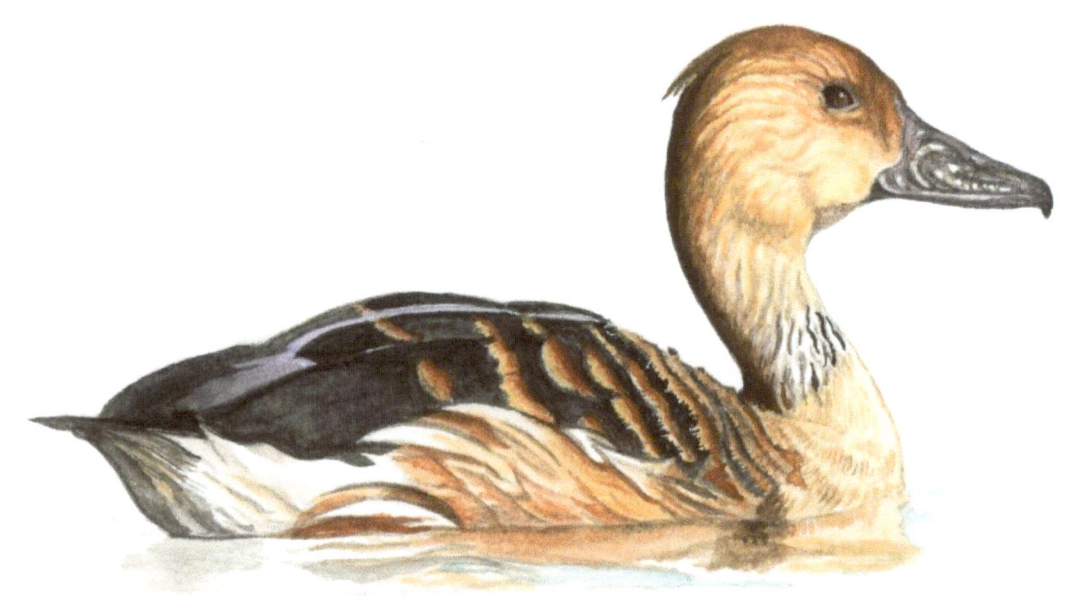

Fulvous Whistling-Duck

Ducks live on every continent (except Antarctica) and on every major island in the world. The duck family includes geese and swans so there are quite a lot of ducks. They are among the earliest domesticated birds. Classified as migratory game birds, ducks have been hunted every year for centuries. Some are endangered, some, like the Labrador Duck, are extinct, and some, like the Trumpeter Swan and the Whistling Swan, were nearly wiped out by the end of the 19th century. Dabbling ducks tip their bodied down to eat aquatic plants on the bottom of shallow water, leaving their tails in the air. Diving ducks arch their backs, then nose on down to swim below the surface. The Ruddy Duck can simply sink slowly without a ripple and the Scaup dives to depths of 20 feet to feed.

Cool Fact: Geese make excellent "watchdogs." They are used to guard businesses, military facilities and private property. Once they are familiarized with who are "their" people or animals, they will challenge all others.

What other birds' names start with D?

E is for Egret
Ardeida

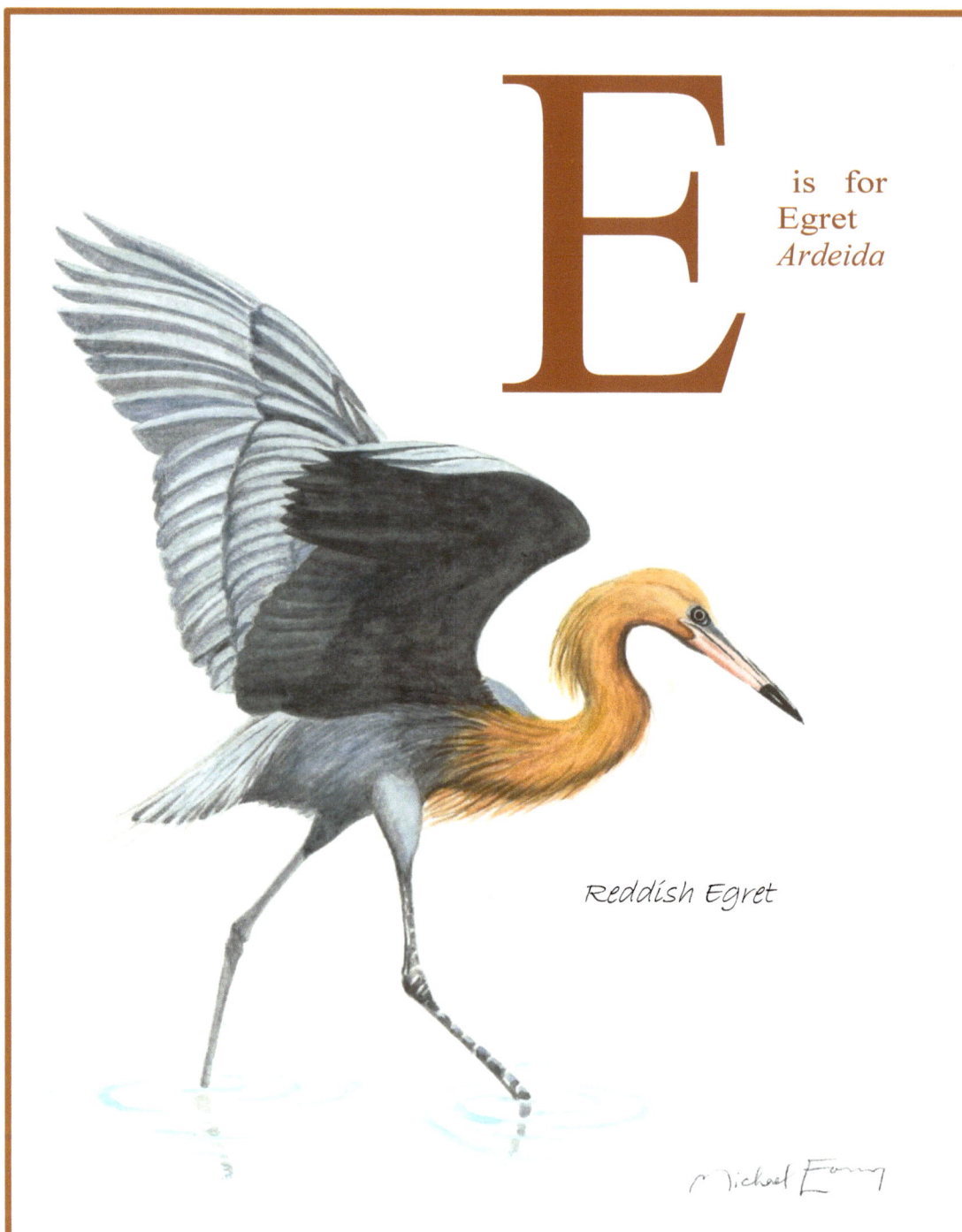

Reddish Egret

Egrets are part of the heron family, which includes bitterns; they are long legged, long-necked wading birds. Except for the Reddish Egret, egrets are snowy white and get their name from the long plumes—aigrettes—for which they were slaughtered in vast numbers. While millions of them were killed annually for food, it was the fashion markets' demand for plumes to decorate women's hair, hats and dresses that devastated bird populations, particularly that of the Great Egret and the Snowy Egret. The flowing white nuptial plumes, grown for the breeding season and then shed, were in such demand that they sold for as much as $32 an ounce in 1903!

Cool Fact: The Audubon Society (named for the great bird painter John James Audubon)—which was instrumental in stopping the plume trade—was founded by George *Bird* Grinnell.

What other birds' names start with E?

F

is for
Flamingo
Phoenicopteridae

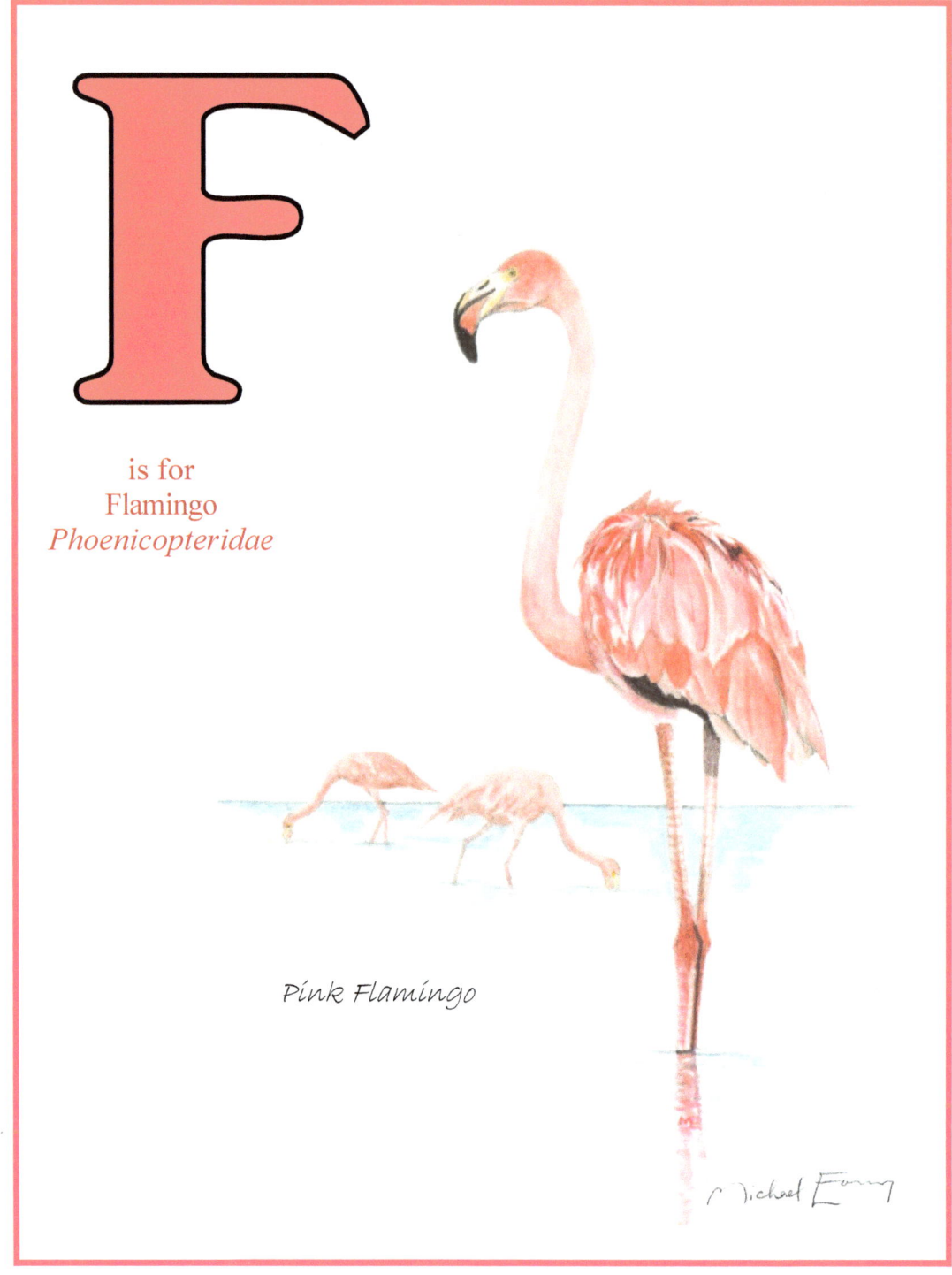

Pink Flamingo

Flamingos are one of the oldest species of birds; they wade in the water with their bill submerged to eat, where it is parallel to the bottom of the lake or pool. Its distinctive downward bent bill identifies this bird. Moving its tongue rapidly back and forth filters water through the tooth-like ridges on the bill. This sieves out the crustaceans, mollusks, insects, tiny fish and vegetation upon which the flamingo lives. Flamingos are found in southern Europe, Africa, northwest India, southwest Asia and in the high Andes of Chile, Peru, Bolivia and Argentina. The American Greater Flamingo, once found in large numbers in Florida, is now rarely seen, although a stray might be spotted in coastal Texas. The closest place to the USA to see them in the wild is the Yucatan, Mexico or Cuba if you can get there. Lawn flamingos are one of the most popular lawn decorations in the USA.

Cool Fact: Carotenoid proteins in the crustaceans that flamingos eat are broken down into pigments which are deposited in growing feathers making them pink or orange.

What other birds' names start with F?

G

is for
Grouse
Tetraonidae

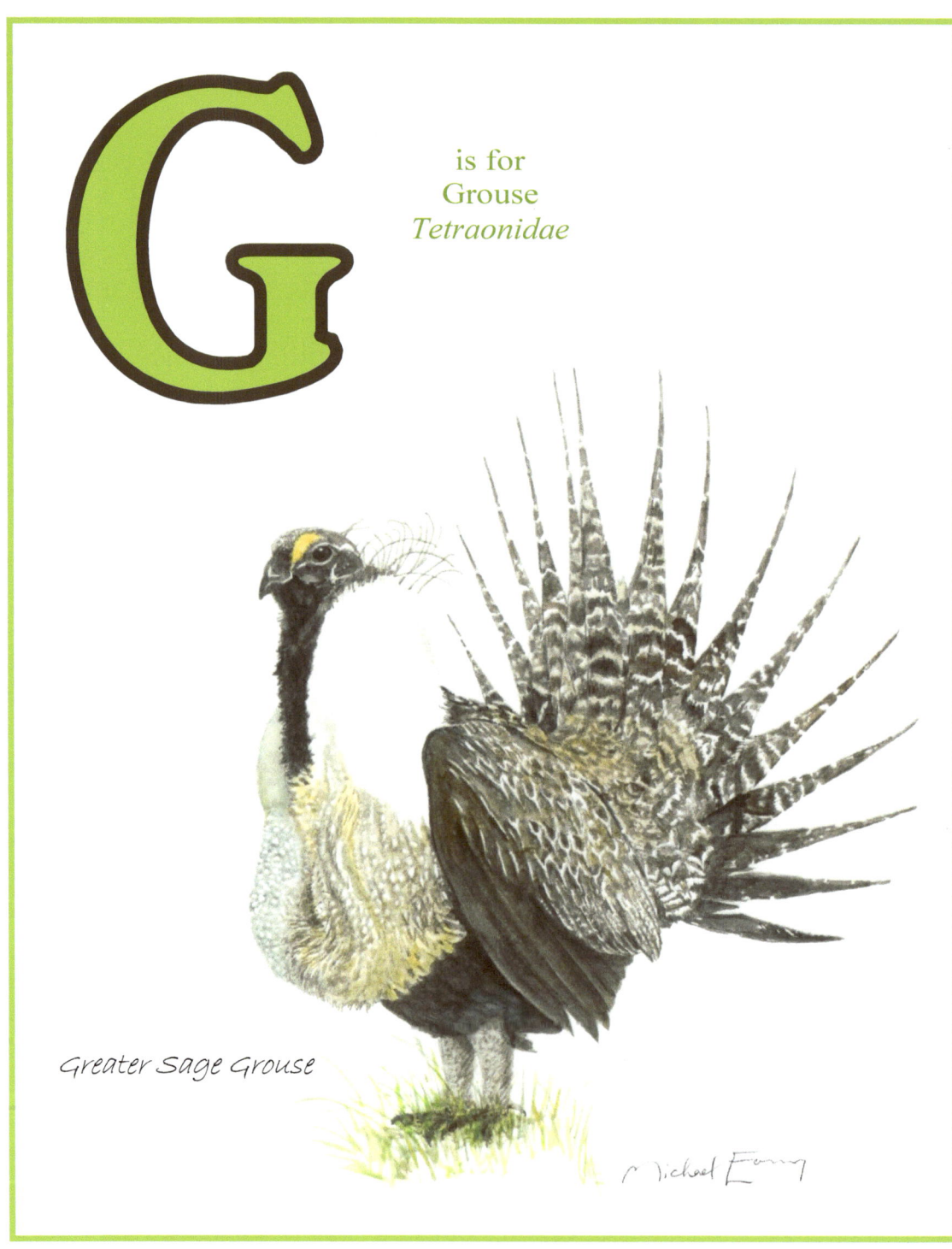

Greater Sage Grouse

Grouse family members include ptarmigan and prairie chicken. All these fowl-like birds have short rounded wings that are good for short rapid flight; generally they prefer to walk. The Greater and Lesser Prairie Chicken, ptarmigan and some other grouse have quite elaborate ceremonial courting habits; inflating bright air sacs, spreading tail feathers, raising ruffs and head feathers and strutting in their dancing grounds. It is the male Sage Grouse though, that has the most spectacular courting display with its large inflating breast air sacs. Once again, loss of habitat and hunting threatens the grouse.

Cool Fact: When ptarmigan go to roost they fly straight into snow banks so as to not leave footprints that predators, such as foxes or lynxes, might follow then catch them while they sleep.

What other birds' names start with G?

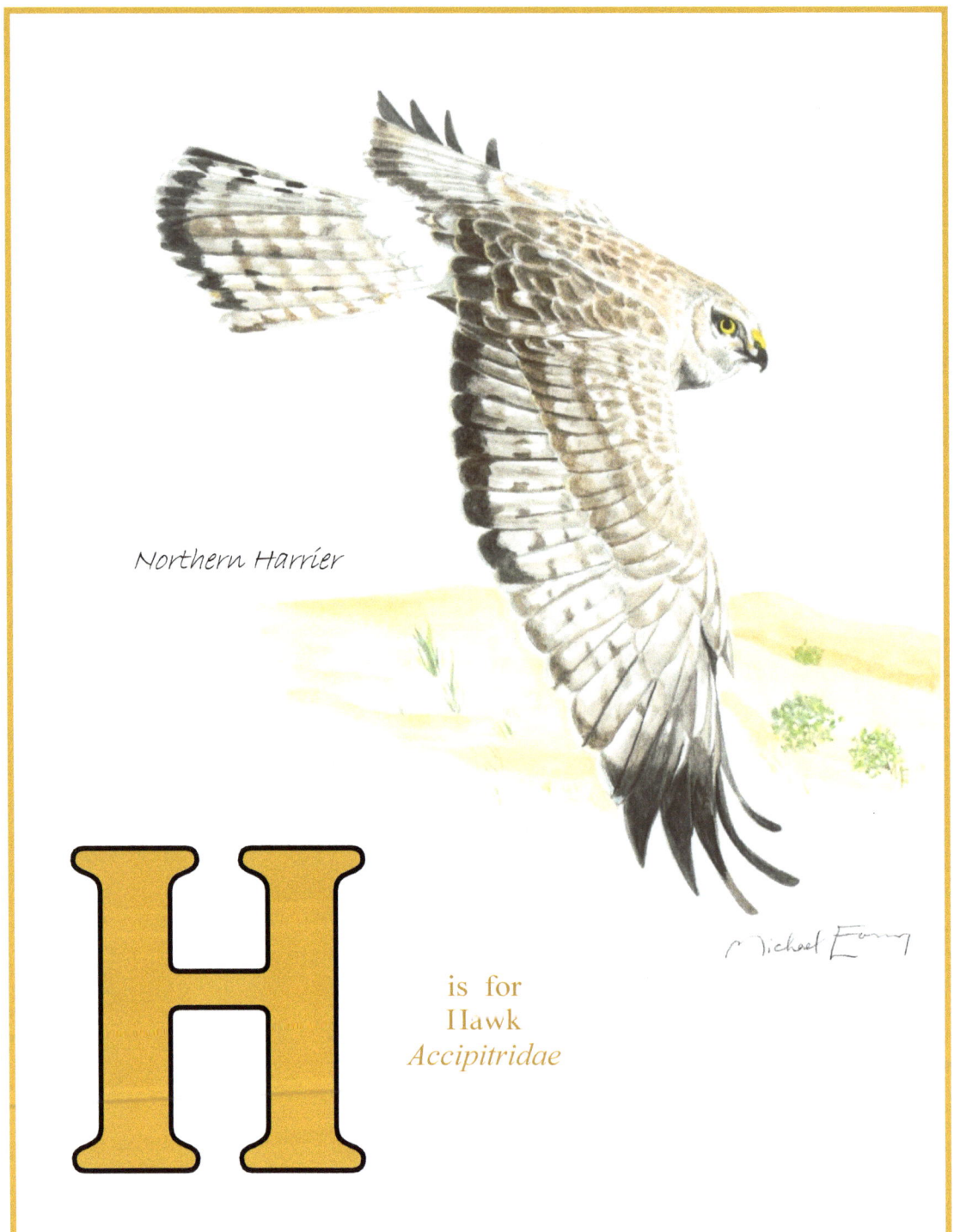

Northern Harrier

H
is for
Hawk
Accipitridae

Hawks are birds of prey. This family includes eagles and kites. Whether swooping down from a great height, hovering just above their prey or cruising low over the ground, like the marsh hawk, their phenomenal eyesight enables them to feed on everything from mice to grasshoppers, gophers, skunks, small birds, snakes, frogs and fish. The Bald Eagle (bald meant white at one time) is the national symbol of the USA and the only eagle unique to North America. It is one of the so-called sea eagles as it will snatch fish from the water. At the top of the food chain, hawks are most vulnerable to toxic chemicals that build up in each link of the chain.

Cool Fact: Diving for prey, the Golden Eagle can reach 150-200 miles per hour!

What other birds' names start with H?

I

is for
Ibis
Threskiornithidae

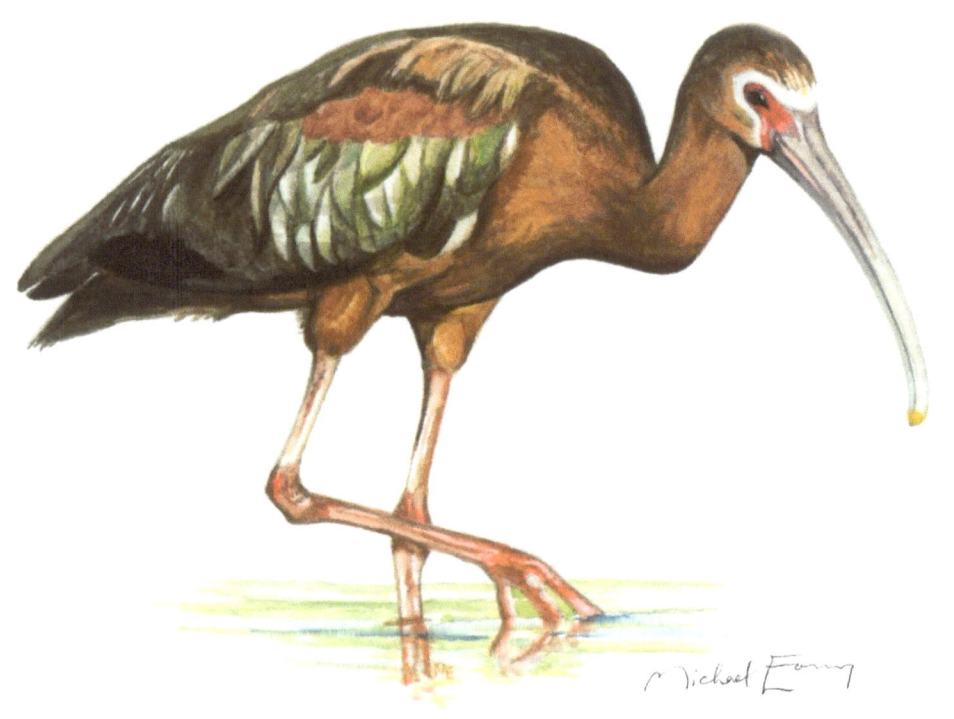

White-faced Ibis

Ibis have been found in tombs! The ancient Egyptians mummified and buried the Sacred Ibis (now extinct in Egypt for almost a century), along with the Pharaohs. There are Old World ibis and New World ibis. The Glossy Ibis made its way across the Atlantic to the Americas and can now be found from the Great Lakes to Texas. Ibis can be seen in groups, probing the ground or waters for beetles, worms, small snakes and slugs. The Roseate Spoonbill is in this family. Its naked head and large spoon-like bill isn't very attractive but its pink color makes it one of the more exotic birds in the waterways and along the coasts of Mexico, Texas and Florida.

Cool Fact: The Scarlet Ibis is the national bird of Trinidad, where it is a protected species.

What other birds' names start with I?

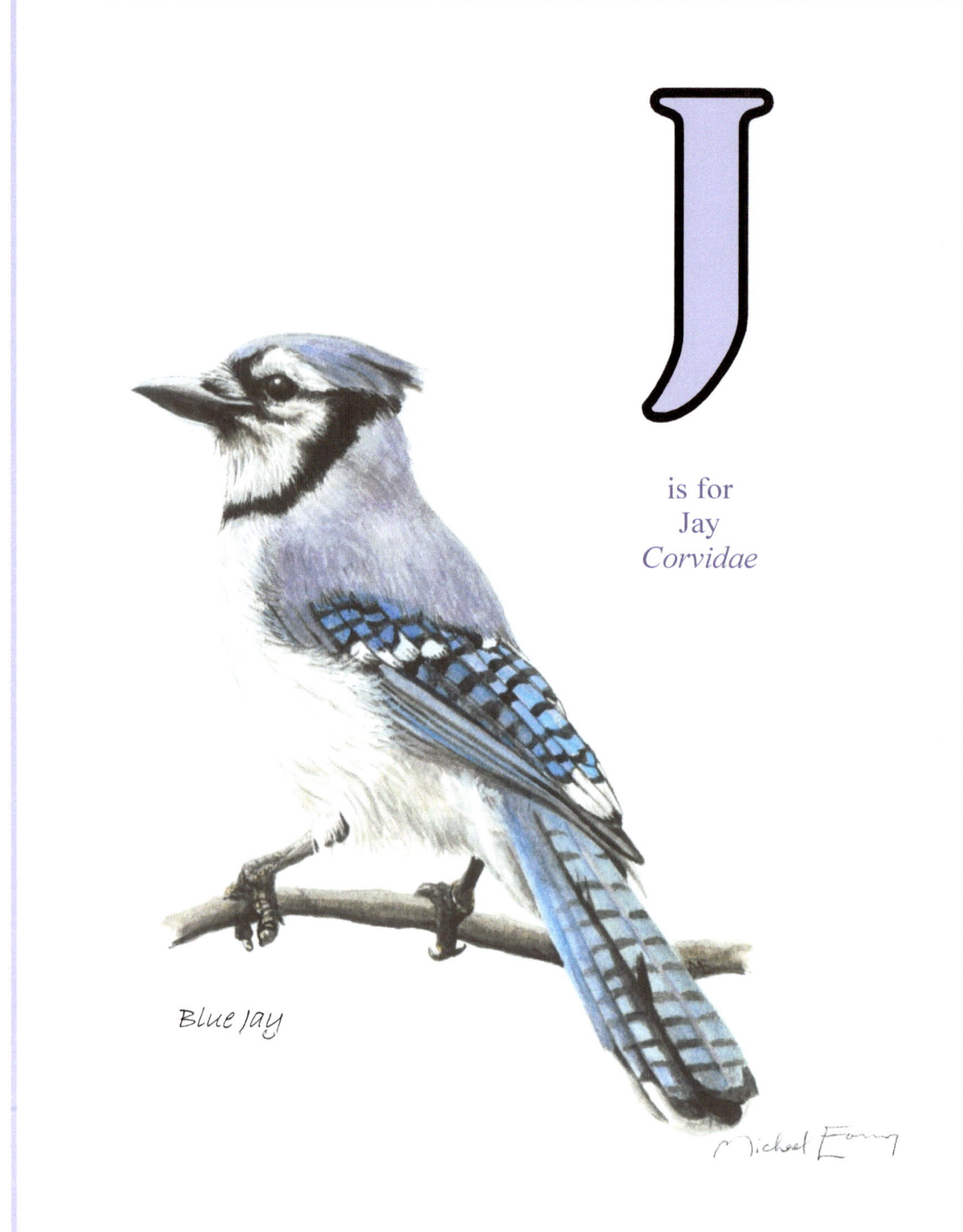

J

is for
Jay
Corvidae

Blue Jay

Jays stand out in more ways than one. There are brown jays, green jays, grey jays and blue jays. Along with the magpies and nutcrackers, jays are the most colorful of the Corvidae family, which also includes ravens and crows. They are all raucous and unmelodious 'talkers.' The Gray Jay is known as 'Whiskey Jack' and 'Camp Robber' for boldly taking items from campsites and hiding them. The Blue Jay and the Scrub Jay bury acorns and other seeds—many of which germinate—making these birds tree-planters. The blue-grey Mexican Jay, like the Green and Brown Jays, sometimes slip across the border into Texas, Arizona and New Mexico. Unlike them, the San Blas Jay is only found on the Pacific slope of west central Mexico.

Cool Fact: The Steller's Jay can imitate other birds like hawks and loons.

What other birds' names start with J?

Green Kingfisher

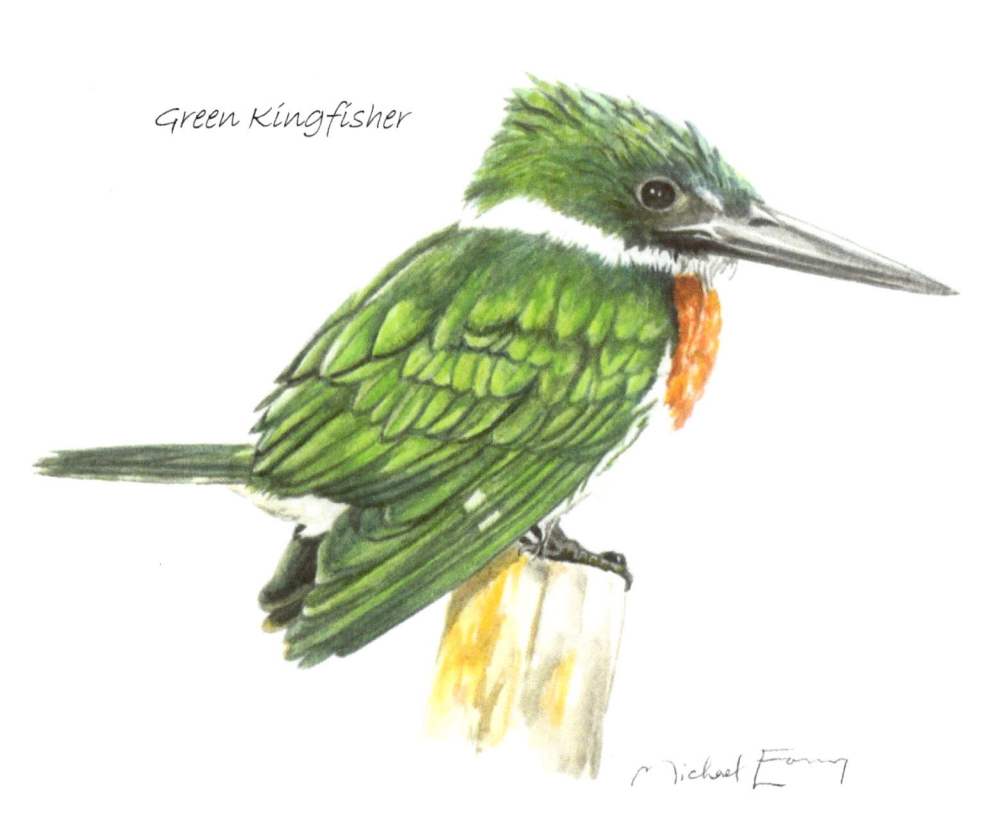

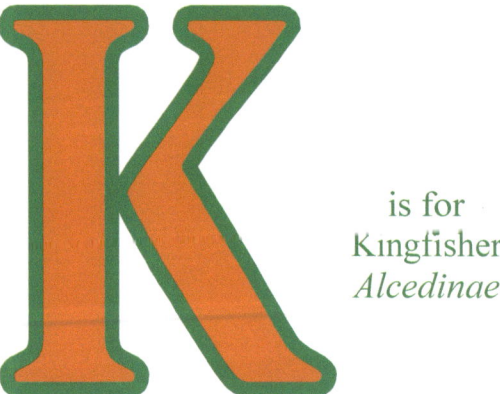

is for
Kingfisher
Alcedinae

Kingfishers are large-headed, mostly chunky, mostly crested, mostly colorful, with iridescent greens, blues and reds. Mostly fish-eating, they watch from overhanging branches or hovering over water then diving in to catch fish, amphibians and aquatic insects. Some kingfishers however, live far from water, eat insects and nest in trees. Most kingfishers burrow into riverbanks to nest. The burrows can be three to seven feet deep and may be lined with clean, white fish bones and scales.

Cool Fact: Halcyone, daughter of Aeolus, Greek god of the wind, with her husband, Ceyx, were turned into kingfishers. The "halcyon days" are when the gods make the winds behave and the seas calm at the time of year when kingfishers were thought to nest at sea (they don't).

What other birds' names start with K?

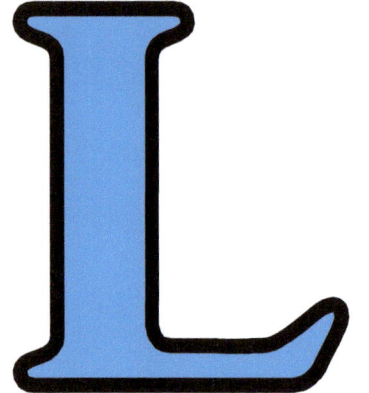

is for
Loon
Gaviidae

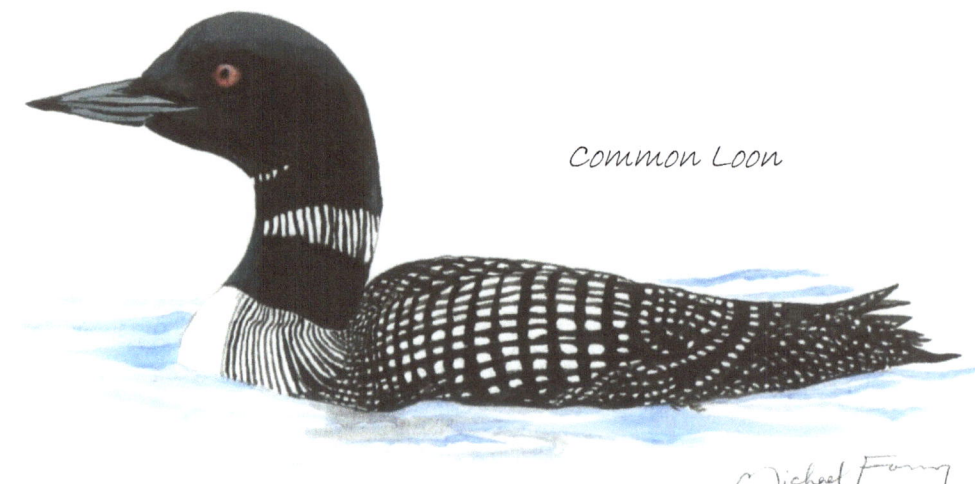

Common Loon

Loons are North American birds though they nest around the world in or near Arctic tundra. There are only four members of this family. The name is thought to come from old Scandinavian 'Lom' meaning lame or clumsy in reference to the fact that, due to the placement of their legs far back on their body, they can scarcely walk on land. They are powerful swimmers underwater, diving to depths of up to 240 feet. By expelling air from their bodies and feathers, they submerge slowly with barely a ripple. Loon chicks ride on the backs of their parents, because their downy feathers are easily soaked and the cold wet could kill them. They appear in the legends and folklore of the Inuit and although known as a northern bird, loons can be seen in the Gulf of Mexico off the Texas and Florida coasts.

Cool Fact: The wails, screams and 'laughter' of this bird have given us the expression, "crazy as a loon."

What other birds' names start with l?

M

is for
Mockingbird
Mimidae

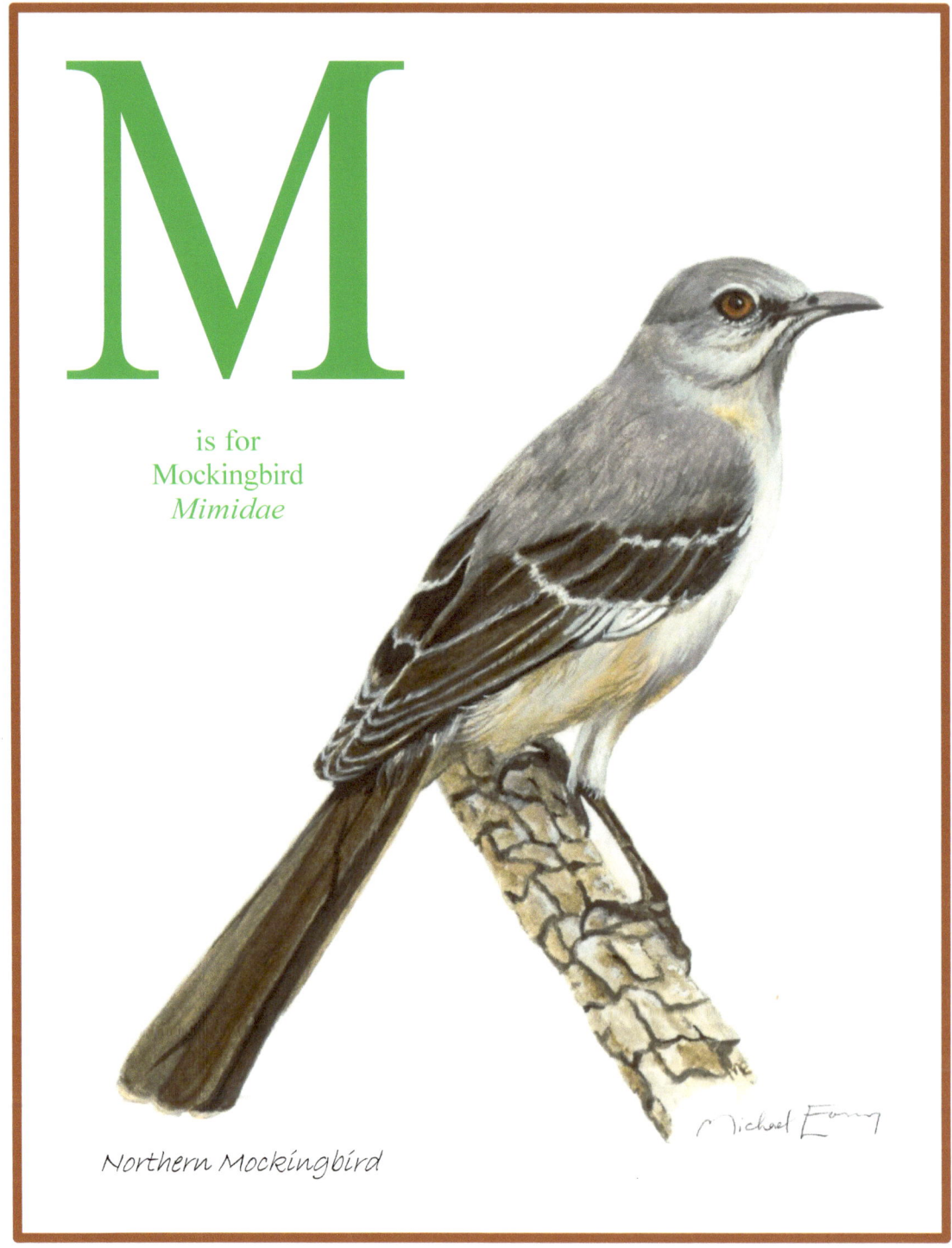

Northern Mockingbird

Mockingbirds might keep you awake at night if you are a light sleeper. This family includes catbirds and thrashers, all of which mimic other birds. The mockingbird is the best, known for imitating everything from the songs of 39 other bird species, to dogs, frogs, crickets and even a piano. The mockingbird is also a great dancer, performing hops, leaps and runs, all the while singing loudly then softly, for hours on end, night and day. The thrashers and catbirds and mockingbirds are mostly ground feeders, rifling through leaves or running down insects. All nest on or within a few feet of the ground. The catbird has learned to recognize the eggs of the parasitic cowbird and throws them out of its nest. The cowbird, like the cuckoo, lays its eggs in other birds' nests.

Cool Fact: *In the catbird seat* means being in a superior or advantageous position, perhaps because the catbird seeks the highest perch from which to sing and display.

What other birds' names start with M?

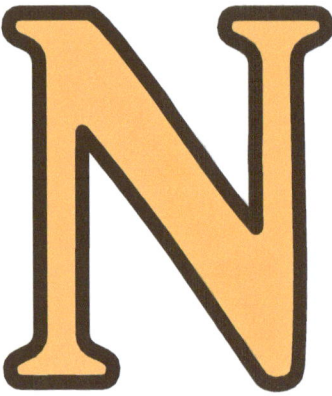

is for
Nightjar
Caprimulgidae

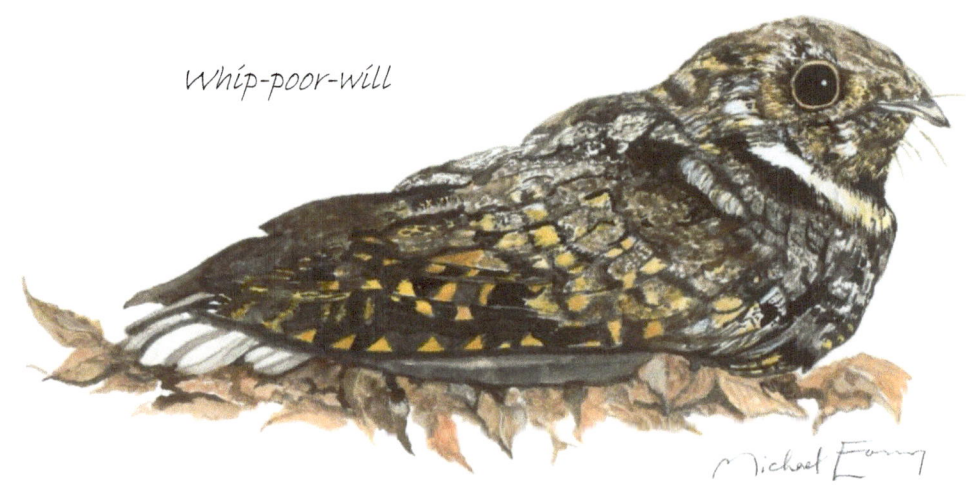

Whip-poor-will

Nightjars can be heard around dusk and into the night or early dawn. Chuck-wills-widow, Poor-will, Whip-poor-will, these names are an approximation of the call they make as is Pauraque, a native Mexican word that sounds like that bird's call. They may be seen sitting in the road or on the ground in fields and woods from where they will silently fly away if disturbed. The nighthawk is the most commonly seen of this family as it swings and swoops, scooping insects up in its capacious mouth—mostly in the evenings or morning—at times creating its characteristic *woof* as it dives.

Cool Fact: Their Latin name comes from *caper*, goat, and *mulgeo*, to milk. It was once believed that these birds sucked milk from goats, so: goatsuckers became their name.

What other birds' names start with N?

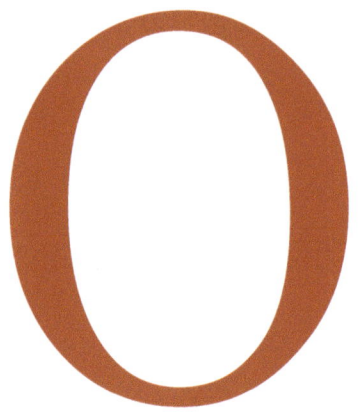

is for
Owl

Strigidae
typical owl
family

And

Tytonidae
barn owl
family

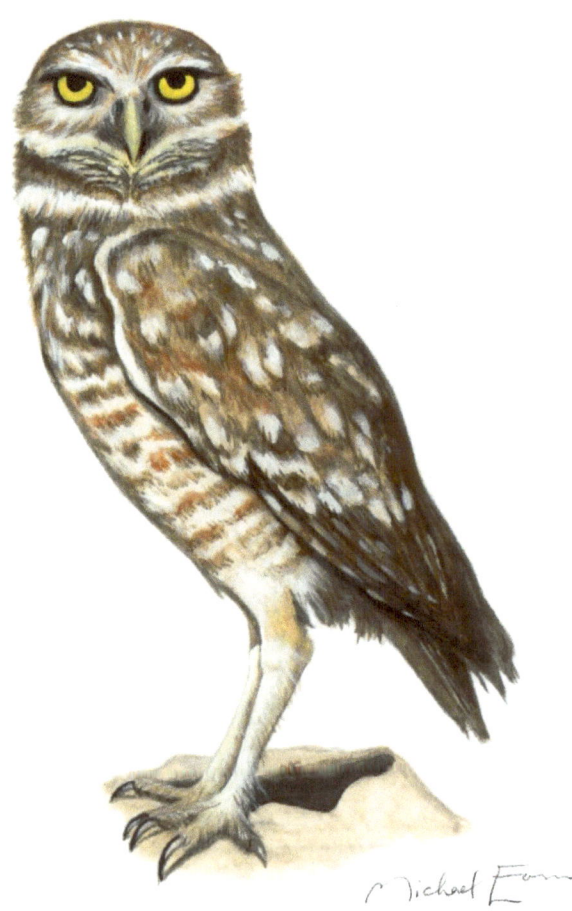

Burrowing Owl

Owls belong in either of the two families. Of these closely related species, the Barn Owl is most easily distinguished by its heart-shaped, disc-like face, while some of the typical owls have ear tufts. Owls usually hunt at night but can hunt by day as well. They fly silently, thanks to the unique construction of their primary wing feathers. The Snowy Owl is one of the largest owls, but the Eurasian Eagle Owl is generally considered the largest in the world. The Saw-whet Owl is smaller than the Screech Owl, and the Elf Owl is the smallest of all. Burrowing Owls take over and enlarge the abandoned burrows of animals such as prairie dogs to fit themselves. All owls have extraordinary sight and hearing.

Cool Fact: The Greek goddess, Athena, and Minerva, the Roman goddess—both goddesses of wisdom—had the owl as their sacred bird. That's why we say, "Wise old owl."

What other birds' names start with O?

P

is for
Pelican
Pelicanidae

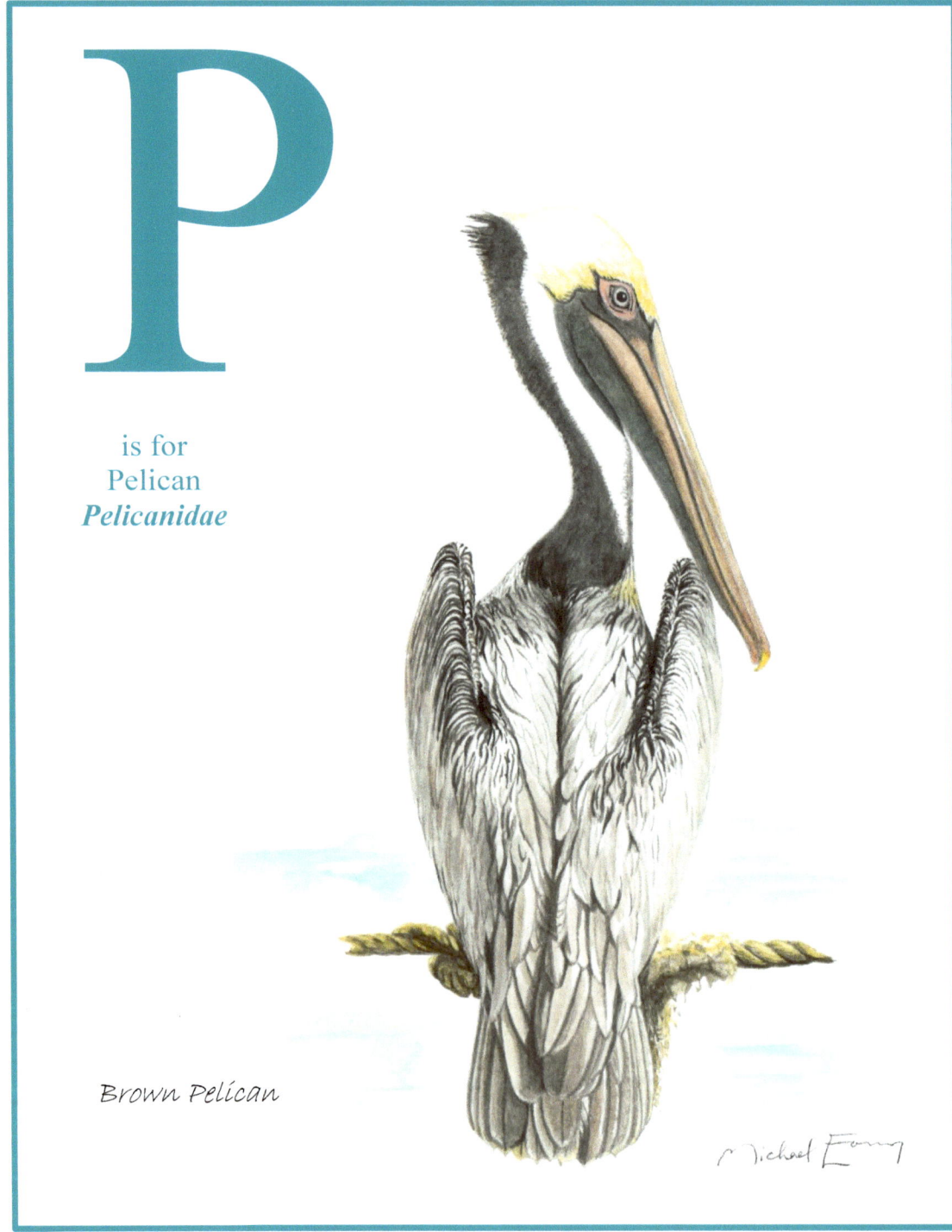

Brown Pelican

Pelicans are among the largest living birds. With their long bills, their large webbed feet, short legs and large bulky bodies, they look clownish, but swimming they look like schooners, and flying they look like seaplanes. The Brown Pelican dives from as high as 70 feet up for a fish, while White Pelicans swim along, often in groups, with their bills in the water to scoop up fish. Pesticide runoff into seawater caused eggshell thinning in Brown Pelicans and they became an endangered species, but with enforced legal restrictions and modifications of many pesticides, they have made a comeback. Nesting pelicans pulsate their pouch, called the gular pouch, to lower their temperature and store partly digested fish for their young to feed right from the pouch.

Cool Fact: As it says in the famous limerick by Edward Lear, "A wonderful bird is the Pelican. His beak can hold more than his belly can. He can hold in his beak enough food for a week! But I'll be darned if I know how the hellican?"

What other birds' names start with P?

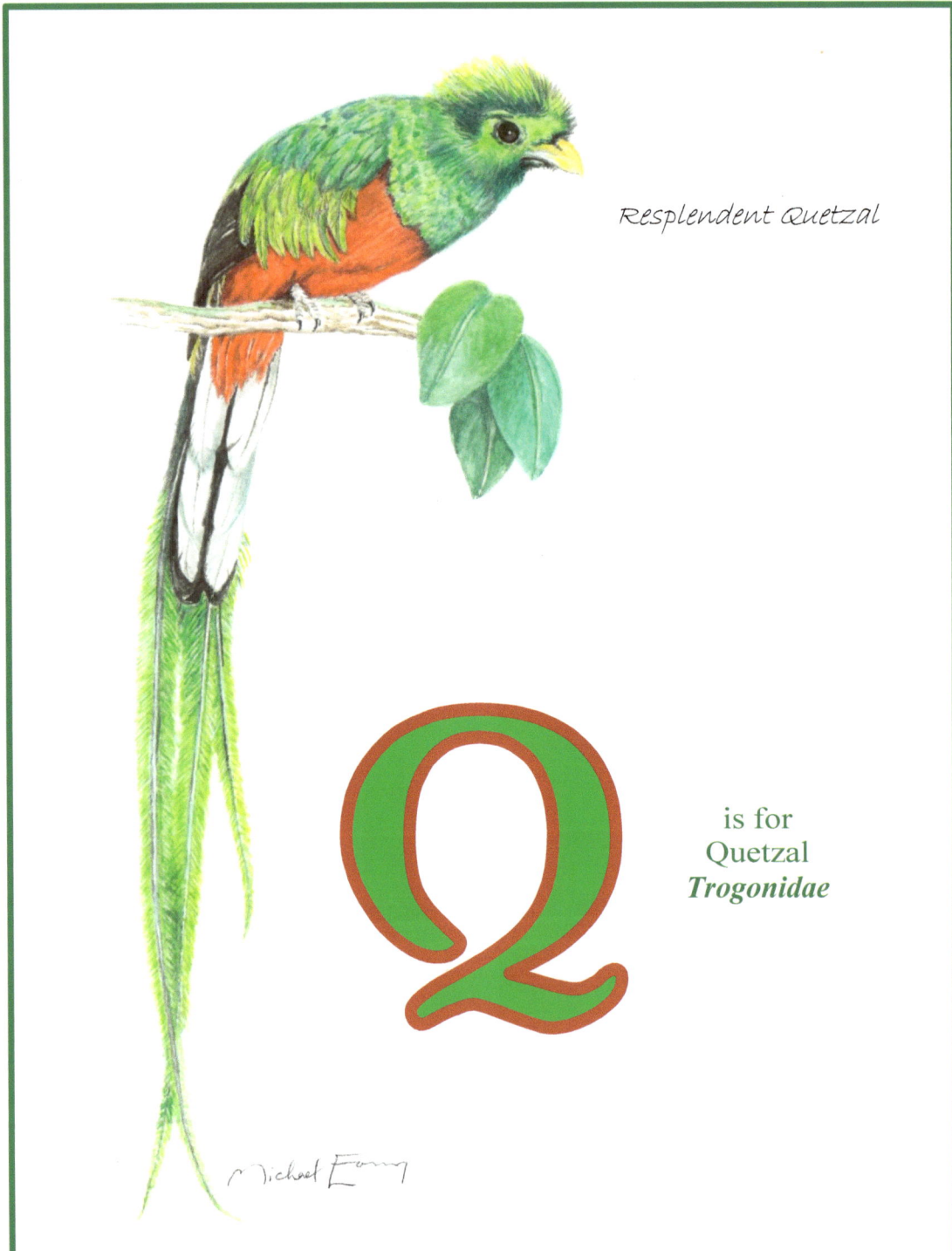

Resplendent Quetzal

is for Quetzal
Trogonidae

Quetzals range from Mexico to northern Bolivia. The Resplendent Quetzal is the national bird of Guatemala and the name of that country's currency. The quetzal is a member of the trogon family—all of whom are beautiful—but the male Resplendent Quetzal, with his vibrant colors and tail up to 36 inches in length, and the Golden-headed Quetzal, are the most striking of the family. The ancient Maya and Aztec rulers wore quetzal feathers during ceremonies and considered the birds, "gods of the air." Others have coveted quetzal feathers to wear, but it is loss of their cloud forest home that is threatening them now.

Cool Fact: A Maya legend says that quetzals sang before the Spanish conquest…but now they only emit a plaintive cry.

What other birds' names start with Q?

R

is for
Rail
Rallidae

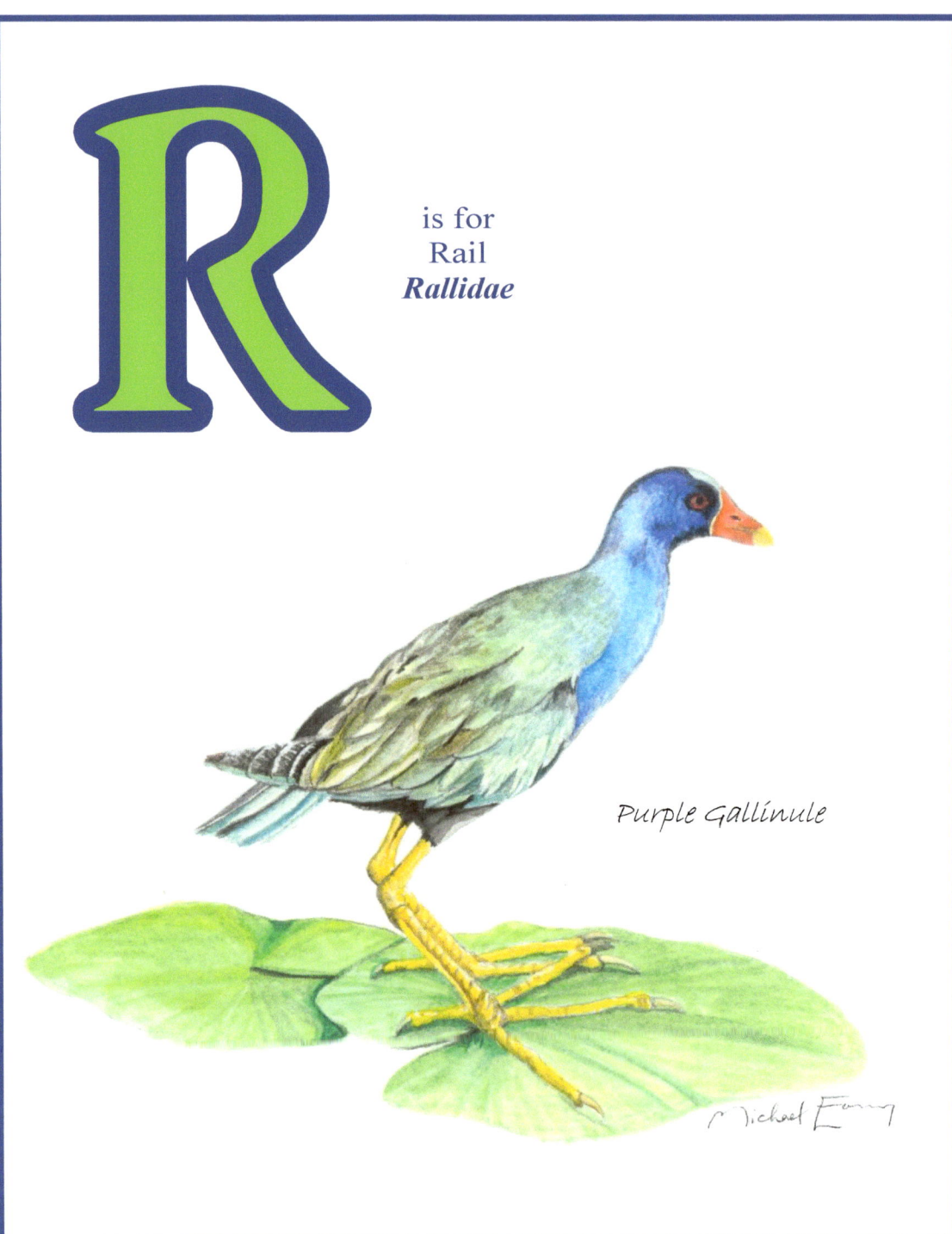

Purple Gallinule

Rails are found worldwide. There are a 130 species, including coots, moorhens, gallinules and soras. Mainly marsh-dwelling, they are secretive and hard to spot. The nine species that nest in North America range from north of New York, south to Florida and Texas, and from California to Massachusetts. Though inclined to stay in the reeds and grasses, many rails migrate long distances. Rails have a claw-like appendage at the tip of the manus (bend of wing) which helps them climb around in dense marsh plants.

Cool Fact: The Black Rail is the smallest rail, but all rails are black when young, which can cause confusion.

What other birds' names start with R?

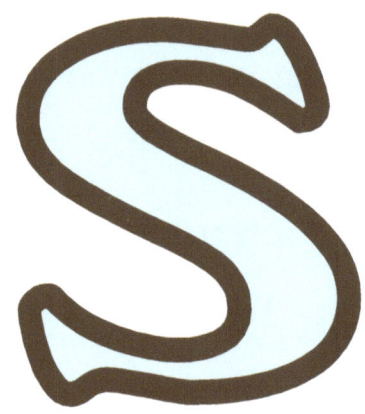

is for
Sandpiper
Scolopacidae

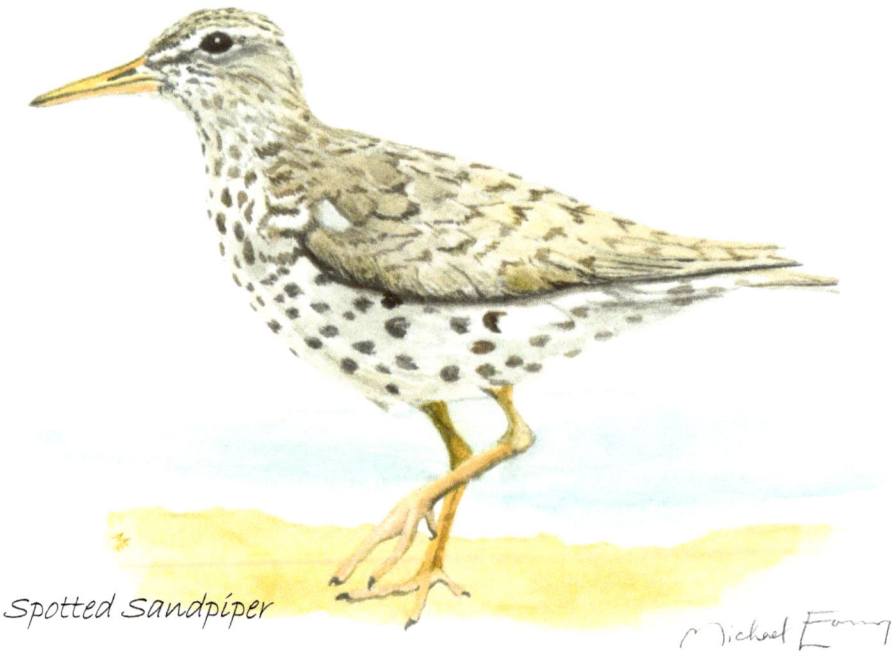

Spotted Sandpiper

Sandpipers, curlews, willets, sanderlings, godwits, snipes and dunlin are all members of the same family. It may have been the sighting of Eskimo Curlews that alerted Christopher Columbus to the fact that land was nearby, though out of sight. Once the Americas were settled, the Eskimo Curlew, along with the Marbled Godwit, Common Snipe, Long-billed Curlew, Red Knot and Buff-breasted Sandpiper were hunted from Argentina to Alaska, almost to extinction. All the members of the sandpiper family are great transcontinental and continental travelers, feeding in marshes, streams and along shorelines.

Cool Fact: The Surfbird is so called because it feeds at the surf line, but it nests as much as a thousand feet above the timberline (over 10,000 feet above sea level).

What other birds' names start with S?

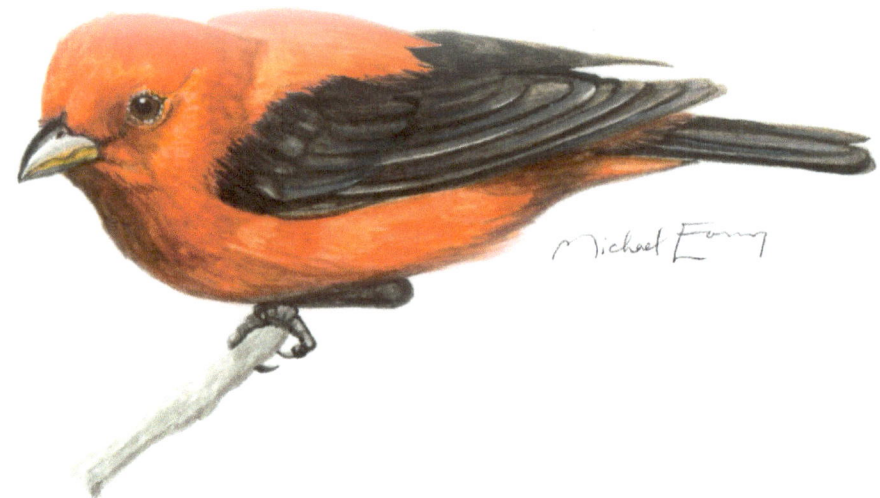

Scarlet Tanager

T

IS FOR
TANAGER
THRAUPIDAE

Tanagers, are limited to the western hemisphere; of the 236 species of tanager only five reach North America. The Blue-gray Tanager and Stripe-headed Tanager have both established themselves in Florida. All eat fruit and insects. The Summer Tanager is called the "beebird" for its liking for bees and wasps, and frequents apiaries in order to pick bees out of the air. The Scarlet Tanager has the dubious distinction of being the tanager most parasitized by the cowbird. Luckily, all other tanagers have a low incidence of this problem.

Cool Fact: A male Western Tanager, picked up after a violent storm, lived in captivity for 15 years and 4 months.

What other birds' names start with T?

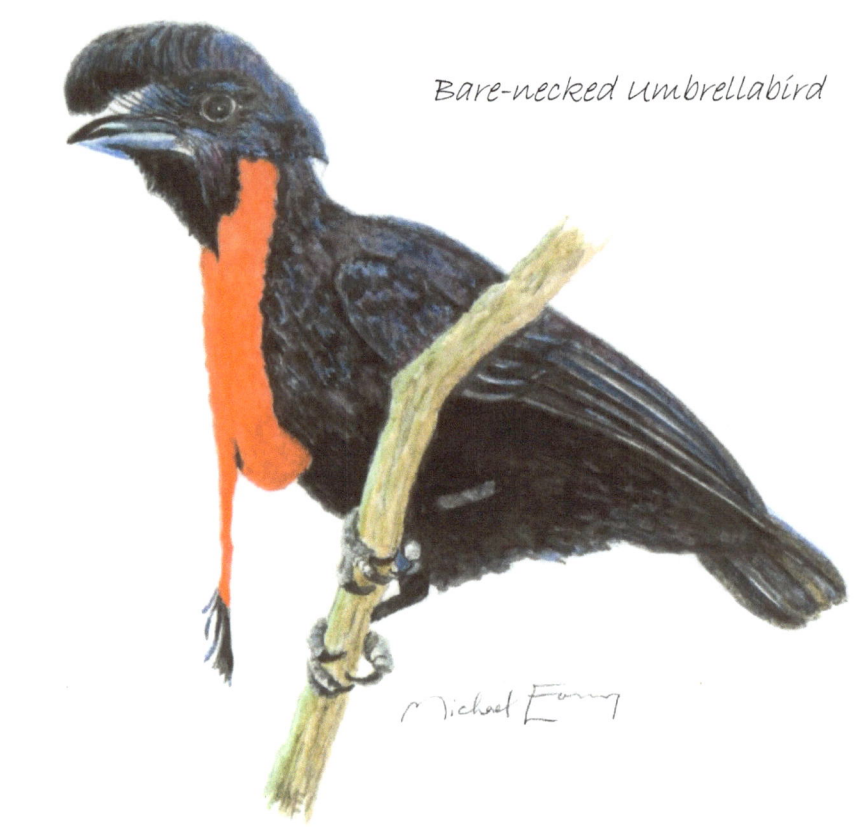

Bare-necked Umbrellabird

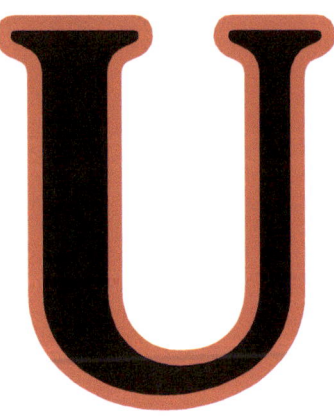

is for
Umbrellabird
Cotingidae

Umbrella birds range from Costa Rica to Argentina and Brazil. Some are very small while others are large and very colorful. The Ornate Umbrellabird is crow-like, eats fruit and lives in the crowns of forest trees. Its retractable crest of black feathers is spread like a parasol in courtship displays. One species has a 13-inch feathered wattle that hangs from its chest; the bird itself is only 18 inches long. Then there is the Bare-necked Umbrellabird. All have inflatable wattles that amplify their loud calls.

Cool Fact: A French ship out of French Guiana was captured by the British. On board was a shipment of brightly colored bird skins intended for Madame Pompadour. George Edwards, a British artist and naturalist, identified one of them as the skin of a cotinga and named it the Pompadour Cotinga.

What other birds' names start with U?

V
is for Vireo
Vireonidae

Black-capped Vireo

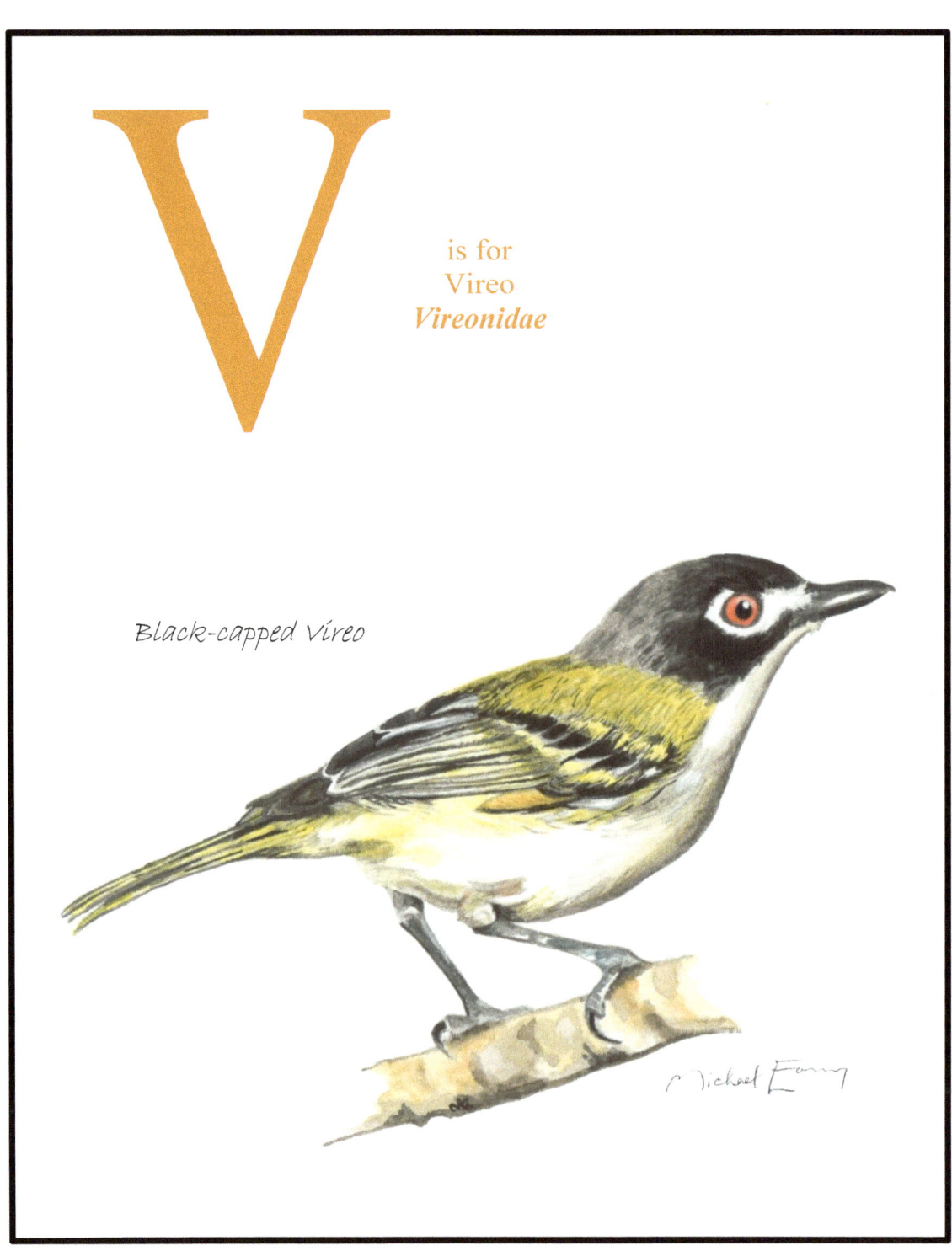

Vireos are believed to have originated in the New World tropics; most vireos winter there, but can be found from Argentina and the West Indies to Canada, where some nest. Some vireos live in the dense mangroves of tropical coasts; others nest as high as nine-thousand feet in the Arizona mountains. Nearly all suspend their nests from the end of slender twigs, using spider silk. The Yellow-throated Vireo builds a very handsome nest; unfortunately, the cowbird finds it a very attractive place to lay its eggs, although the Red-eyed Vireo suffers most from this invader. Listen for the male Warbling-vireo's simple melody as it sings hour after hour from spring into September.

Cool Fact: A Red-eyed Vireo sang 22,197 songs in a 10-hour summer day, a possible record by a North American bird.

What other birds' names start with V?

W

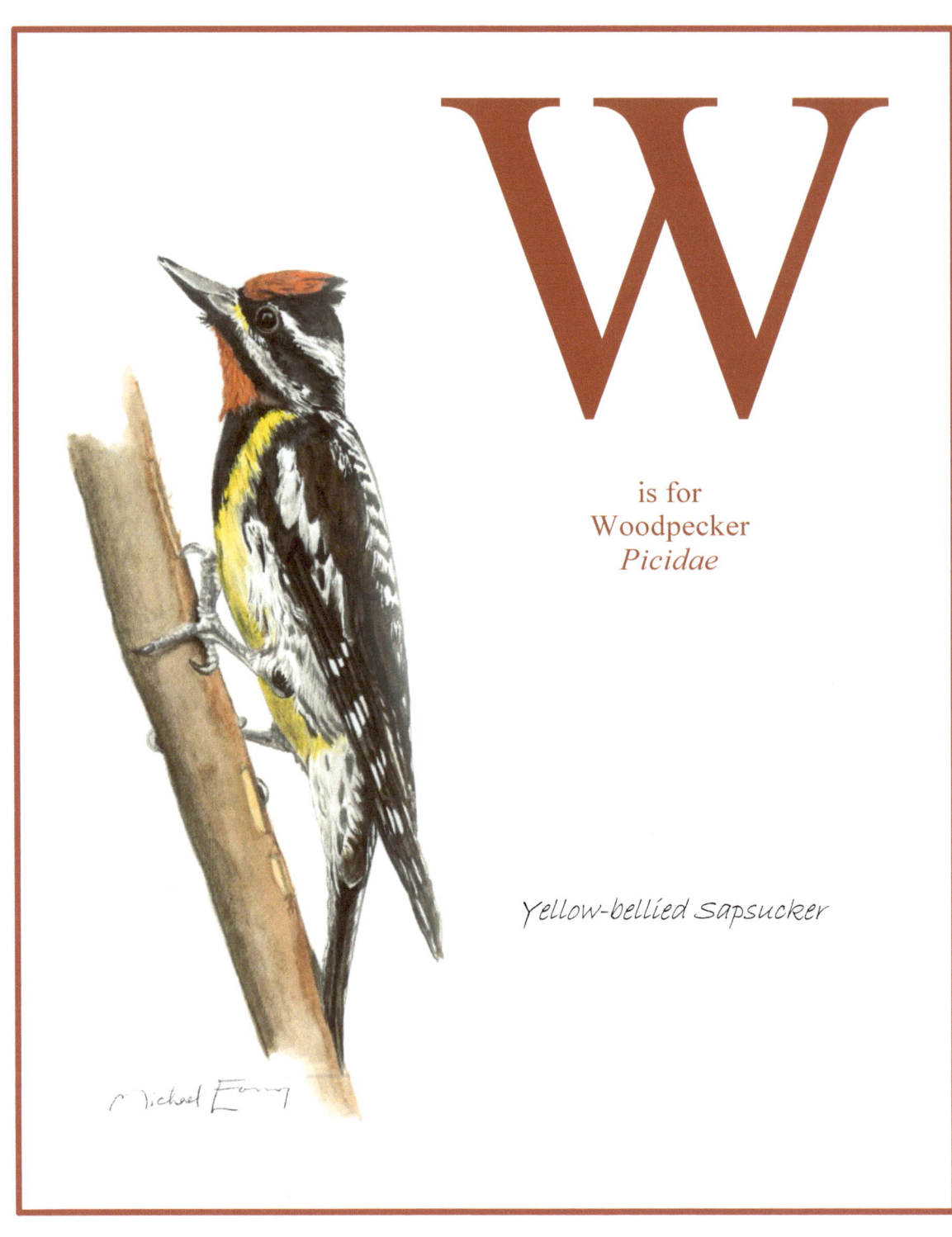

is for
Woodpecker
Picidae

Yellow-bellied Sapsucker

Woodpeckers, sapsuckers and flickers are in the same family. Most woodpeckers have four toes, some three, with which they cling to the trunks of trees, propped up by their strong tail feathers. The woodpecker's straight, hard, pointed bill is used to chisel or hack into the bark and wood of trees as it searches for insects, beetles or their larvae. Strong muscles of the thick-walled skull, together with a space between the brain's tough outer membrane and the brain itself, absorb the shock of this activity. Flickers often eat on the ground. They can extend their long, sticky tongues into anthills for their favorite food. Sapsuckers tap trees for their sap and also eat the insects attracted to the oozing sap.

Cool Fact: The Acorn Woodpecker stores acorns and other nuts in tight individual holes it makes in tree trunks. One large sycamore in California was found to have 20,000 acorns embedded in its trunk, left there by a woodpecker.

What other birds' names start with W?

X
is for
Extinct
Exstinctus

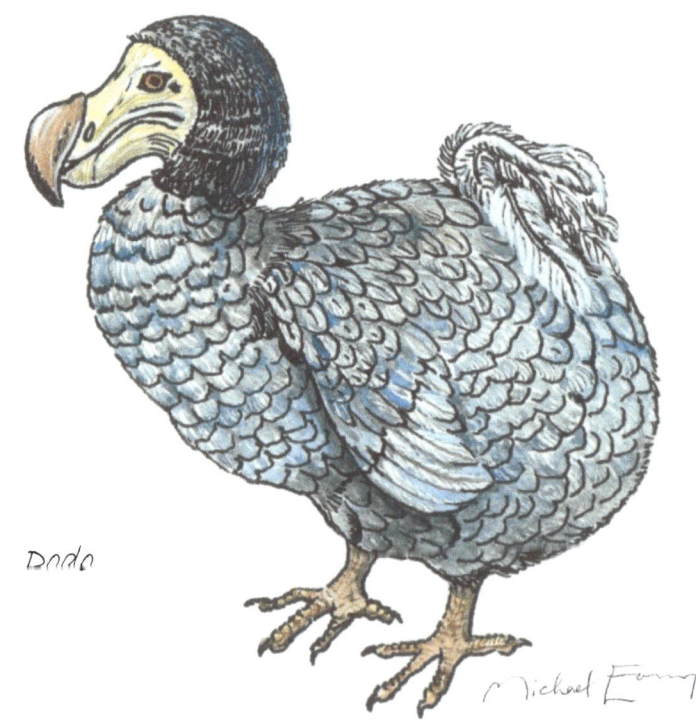

Dodo

X'd out, that has been the fate of many species. The Dodo and the Passenger Pigeon are probably the best known birds to have become extinct due to human hunting, but many others have disappeared through loss of habitat due to human population growth, deforestation, farming or other land use…at least this is true in North America which has the worst record of all the continents. Hawaii and Guam have lost most of their native species due to the introduction by man of exotic species. Since the year 1500, over 190 species of birds have become extinct. 1200 species are currently considered to be endangered or threatened. The Ivory-billed Woodpecker is thought to be extinct, but may still survive in Cuba.

Cool Fact: During the last ten years many new species of birds have been discovered in Brazil, Colombia, Peru and Indonesia. In 2003 a forest partridge was found and named *Xenoperdix udzungwensis*. Now we have an "X" bird!

What other birds' names start with X?

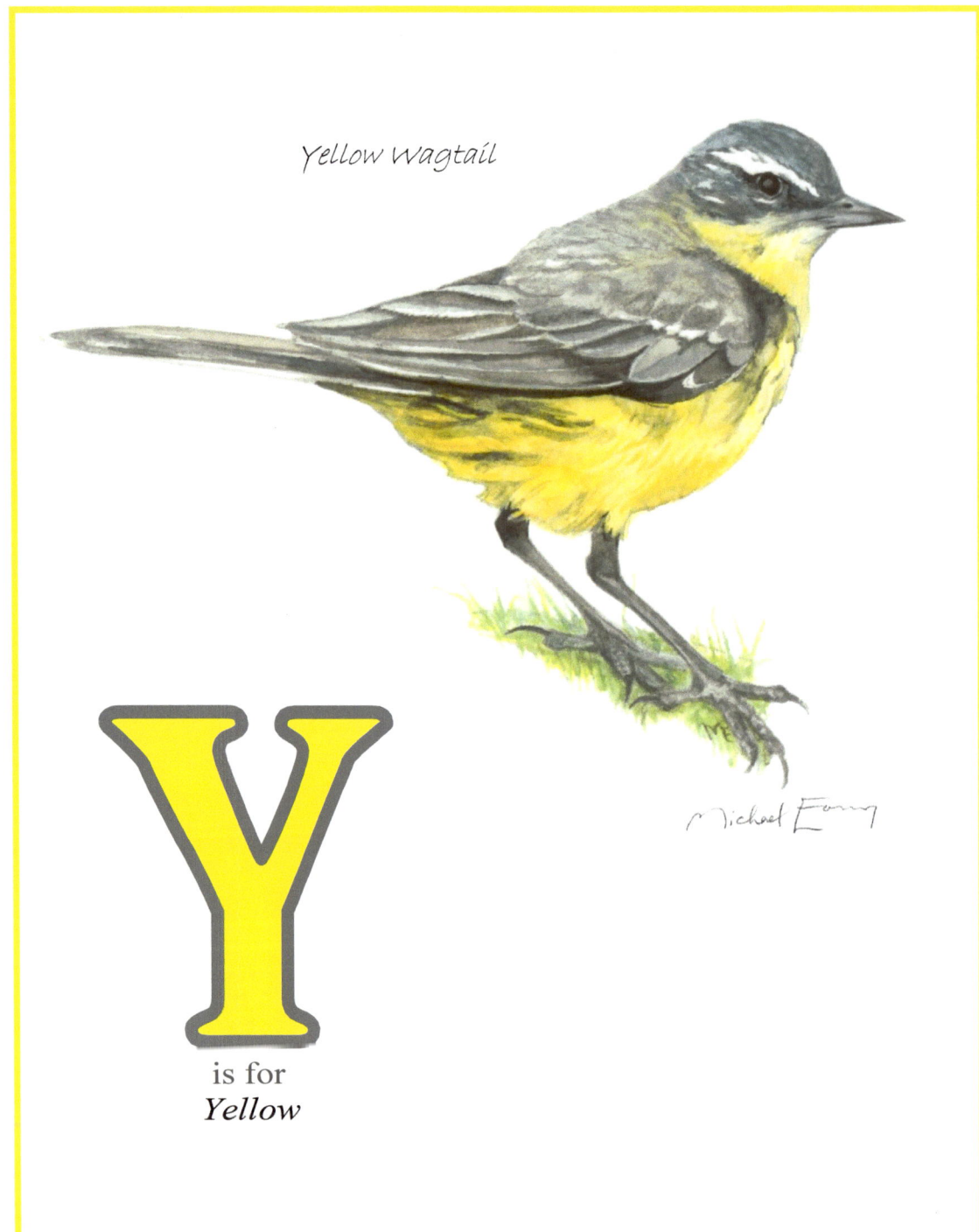

Yellow Wagtail

Y is for *Yellow*

Yellowlegs, the Greater and the Lesser, are in the sandpiper family. The Yellowhammer is in the bunting family. There is also a Yellow Warbler and a Yellow-browed Warbler; a Yellow-billed Cuckoo, a Yellow-breasted Chat and a Yellow-bellied Sapsucker, a Yellow Wagtail and a Yellow-breasted Sunbird, but no bird family whose name begins with "Y."

Cool Fact: When a ground predator, or a human, approaches Yellow Wagtails, several males will fly up and circle the intruder.

What other birds have yellow coloring?

Z

is for
Zonotrichia

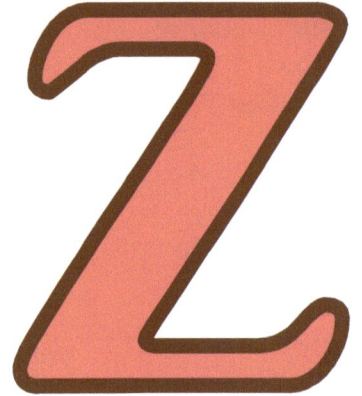

White-crowned Sparrow

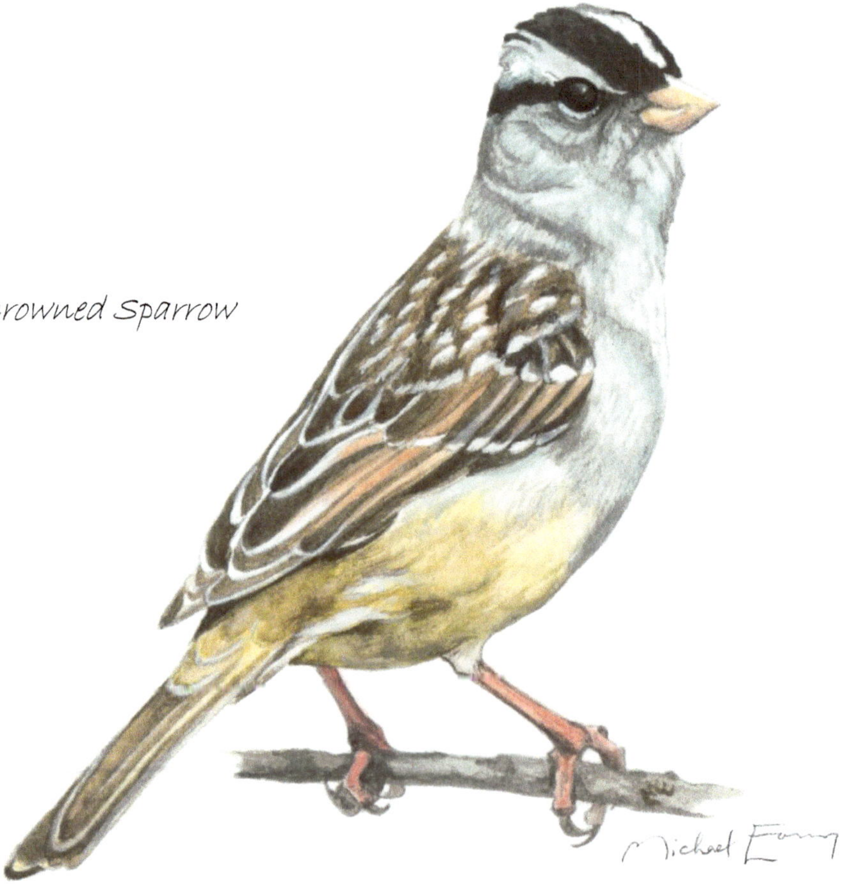

Zonotrichia is the genus name for five species of sparrows; it includes: the Harris's Sparrow, named by John James Audubon for Edward Harris, who accompanied him on his Missouri River expedition in 1843, the Golden-crowned Sparrow which lives along the Pacific coast of North America from Alaska to Baja California, and the Rufous-collared Sparrow that lives in South America. The song of the White-throated Sparrow, which lives in the Canadian wilderness, has been rendered as "Old Sam Peabody, Peabody, Peabody" and as "Pure sweet Canada, Canada, Canada." The White-crowned Sparrow can be found all over continental USA, but is most abundant in the west. Several hundred of them were trapped in San Jose, California then released in Maryland as an experiment. One year later they had returned to San Jose.

Cool Fact: While at the Philadelphia Academy of Natural Science, Charles Bonaparte named the *Zenaida* Dove for his wife. She was Zenaide Charlotte Julie Bonaparte, daughter of the King of Spain (1803-1813) and niece of Napoleon Bonaparte.

What other birds' names start with Z?

Do you quail (cringe, flinch, recoil or wince) at the idea of having to think of more bird names? Well, here's a bonus and a list to help you. The Bobwhite quail says, "Bob Whiiite!" The black-and-white face pattern of the male Montezuma Quail makes him look a little clownish.

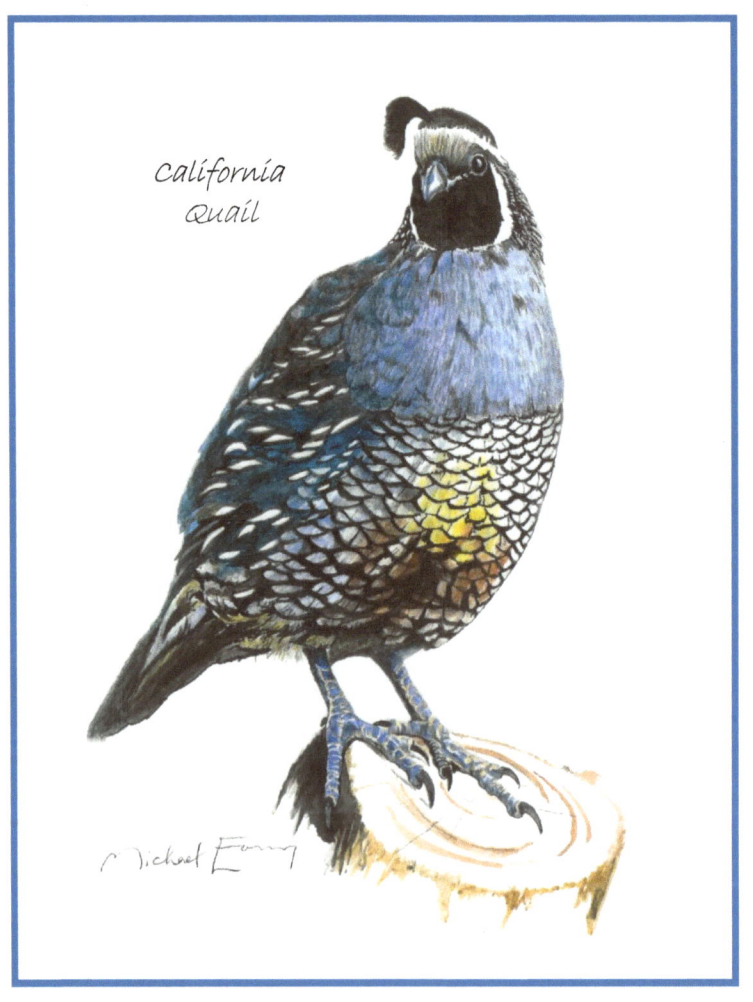

California Quail

More A to Z birds:

A. Avocet, Anhinga, Auk
B. Bunting, Bulbul, Bittern
C. Cassowary, Crow, Chickadee
D. Dove, Dickcissel, Dipper
E. Eagle, Eider
F. Falcon, Finch, Flycatcher, Frigatebird
G. Grosbeak, Grebe, Gnatcatcher
H. Heron, Hummingbird
I. Io, Iiwi
J. Junco, Jaeger, Jackdaw
K. Kite, Kildeer, Kookaburra
L. Lark, Lapwing, Lyrebird
M. Myna, Moorhen, Murrelet
N. Nuthatch, Nightingale, Noddy
O. Oriole, Ostrich, Oystercatcher
P. Petrel, Parrot, Pheasant
Q. Queen Whydah, Quaker Parakeet
R. Roadrunner, Redstart, Ruff
S. Shrike, Skua, Swallow
T. Turkey, Tern, Towhee
U. Ula-ai-hawane, Upupidae, *Uria aalge*
V. Vulture, Veery, Verdin
W. Waxwing, Wagtail, Wigeon
X. Xantus's Murrelet
Y. Yellowthroat
Z. *Zoothera*

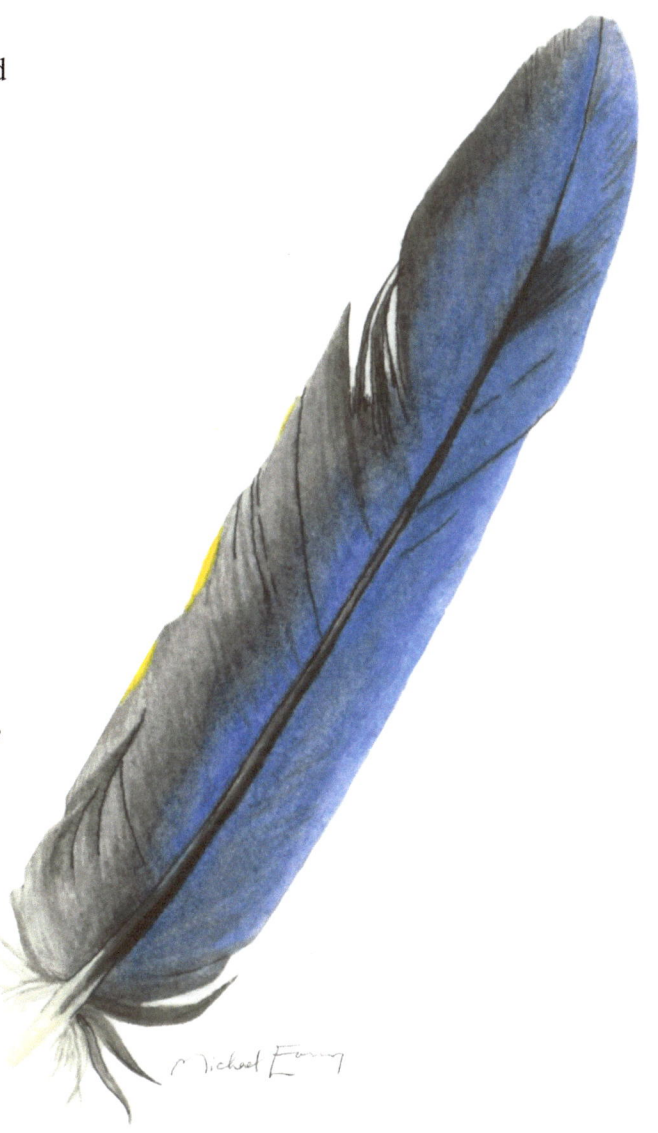

Bibliography:

<u>Field Guide to the Birds of North America</u>, National Geographic Society

<u>Field Guide to the Birds of Australia</u>, by Graham Pizzey, Collins Publishing

<u>The Audubon Society Encyclopedia of North American Birds</u>, by John K. Terres, Wing Books Publishing

<u>The Birds of Britain and Europe</u>, by Herman Heinzel, Richard Fitter, John Parslow, Collins Publishing

<u>National Audubon Society Field Guide to North American Birds</u>, by Miklos D. F. Udvardy, Knopf

<u>Wikipedia</u>

<u>Birds of North America</u>, by Tom Woods, Sheri Williamson and Jeffrey Glassberg, Sterling Publishing

American Museum of Natural History
<u>Birds of North America</u>, by Francoix Villeumier, Editor-in-Chief
<u>Smithsonian Q & A Birds</u>, by Christina Wilson, Collins Publishing <u>The A.O.U. Check-List of North American Birds</u>, American Ornithologists' Union (1998)

<u>Handbook of the Birds of the World</u>, Lynx Edicions (1992)

If you enjoyed this book, Michael P. Earney would be most appreciative if you would leave a review on Amazon, Goodreads, or any other Review site you like.

Also, don't forget to tell your friends!
Word of mouth advertising is the most precious Thank You,
a reader could give to an author.

Visit www.MichaelEarney.com to learn more about this author's books
and various achievements.

www.ingramcontent.com/pod-product-compliance
Lightning Source LLC
Chambersburg PA
CBHW051207220526
45473CB00003B/942